S0-AFV-577

THE CHRISTIAN TRADITION

AND THE

UNITY WE SEEK

THE CHRISTIAN TRADITION AND THE UNITY WE SEEK

GIVEN AS RICHARD LECTURES AT THE UNIVERSITY OF VIRGINIA IN CHARLOTTESVILLE, VIRGINIA, BY

Albert C. Outler

NEW YORK *Oxford University Press* 1957

LIBRARY OF CONGRESS CATALOGUE CARD NUMBER: 57–10386

PRINTED IN THE UNITED STATES OF AMERICA

TO MY FATHER

My first witness to the Christian Tradition

PREFACE

THESE lectures are offered as a tract for the times—no more and, I hope, no less. They are concerned with some of the problems and prospects of Christian unity and they seek to stress the unity and continuity of the Christian tradition in the common history which even separated Christians have, as joint heirs with Jesus Christ and members of His Body, the Church.

It is an open secret that the ecumenical movement has, in recent years, lost some of its earlier momentum—more because of the extreme difficulty of the residual problems it faces than from the failure of nerve among its devoted advocates. But these advocates are still too few—and they still tend to be bunched somewhat too closely in a sort of ecumenical coterie. There are still vast segments of Protestant Christianity—denominational officials, pastors, laymen—who are not much more than nominally committed to the ecumenical movement and its aims. This is due largely, of course, to their lack of significant ecumenical experience but this very lack tends to be self-maintaining.

We have been saying for a long time that we must broaden the base of ecumenical participation—and notable efforts in this direction have produced important, though spotty, results. Yet the urgency of the situation grows more acute. The ecumenical cause needs a new burst of vitality and support—and this must come from the broad, mid-range leadership of the churches, and especially, I think, from the rising generation of pastors and lay leaders who have 'discovered' the ecumenical movement in the seminaries and universities. Failing some such reinvigoration, there is grave danger that the movement will presently falter in its forward motion, and a supremely significant 'fullness of time' will pass unransomed. Many hands and hearts are straining at just this task—and this little book is proffered as another contribution to this common effort.

The American university is disposed, in all its natural instincts, to favor ecumenical endeavors of various sorts. It is committed, at least in principle, to the unity of knowledge and to persuasion as the basic method of social change. In the last two decades, it has witnessed an uncommon revival of interest in 'religion in higher education' and it has been long familiar with interdenominational patterns of religious activities. And yet it cannot be claimed that very many academic men really understand the *distinctive* concerns of the modern ecumenical movement or recognize the link between the all-too-halfhearted co-operation between divided Christians in a campus community and the tremendous adventure and enterprise of the World Council of Churches. Because he naturally favors co-operation over partisanship, the Christian academic is almost certain to approve the quest for Christian unity. Yet, typically, he knows much too little about the matter and is not vitally engaged by the difficulties and opportunities which confront us now so imperatively. Here, then, is one of the most fruitful fields for new enlistments in the ecumenical cause.

This hope and conviction were so strong for me that when the University of Virginia honored me with an invitation to deliver the Richard Lectures in 1955, I felt emboldened to broach this topic to a general university audience. Their interest and gracious response have encouraged me to offer the lectures to a wider public. I do so in the belief that there is a great opening frontier in the vast throng of younger leaders in our schools and churches who are willing to affirm and promote the ecumenical enterprise if they can only come to understand what is involved in it and what is required of them. Our churches, by virtue of their covenant in the World Council of Churches, have an urgent obligation to guide such people toward such an understanding.

This book seeks to stress three points: the Christian *community;* the *continuity* of this community in history; and the centrality, in this community and this history, of Jesus Christ—God's '*tradition*' to human history which redeems it. Such a perspective as this, I believe, will allow us then to consider both the nature of the unity we seek—a perennial, yet presently crucial, concern of the ecumenical movement—and the right means and spirit in which to move forward toward it.

The veteran 'ecumaniac' may expect to find much here that is familiar—though I hope he will recognize some new departures from the established conventions of ecumenical apologetics. In particular, I hope he will give some attention to the emphasis upon the essential unity of the Christian Scriptures and the Christian tradition (Chapter four). He will, of course, recognize how deeply I am indebted to the great pioneers of the movement and to the enormous bibliography it has produced.

Historians and theologians will quickly notice that I have made no great effort to brace some rather large generalizations and conclusions with the proper webbing of references and citations. If they are charitably inclined, they will realize that this seemed unprofitable in this particular undertaking—and so will pass their judgments on the validity of the arguments rather than on their apparatus. It goes without saying, however, that the cause to which the book is devoted will be served if its errors and misinterpretations are pointed out—and corrected.

Readers with neat minds will recognize soon enough that some of the basic terms in my argument (e.g. 'community' and 'tradition') are insufficiently defined. I have some hopes, however, that the more perceptive ones will see that this has been, in part at least, deliberate. My chief concern here is to establish a perspective, to describe the ecumenical atmosphere, to enlist the reader in a wrestle for himself with the problem of the Christian community and its central tradition. I have felt that it would be both premature and distracting to propose my own answers as targets for critics who have not yet been caught up into the current mood of ecumenical conversation. If my general thesis is in any way acceptable, then certainly the more formidable task of rigorous analysis is in order. But it is a part of that thesis that contention over prior definitions is not very fruitful until it takes place within the perspective of prior community. For now, at least, I shall be well content if this book can serve to stimulate the kind of understanding and interest that will then proceed on its own toward more definitive answers to the main problems adumbrated here: the common history of the Christian community, the single and central tradition of that community, and the Christian theology of history.

My thanks are due to many who have helped in so many ways in this modest venture. Professors Edward

Younger and Vernon MacCasland were my hosts at the University of Virginia, and were unfailingly hospitable and helpful. When the lectures were given, in slightly revised form, at the Spring Convocation of the Washington Council of Churches in 1956, Acting Dean Calvin Keene of The School of Religion of Howard University and Professor Albert Mollegen of the Virginia Episcopal Seminary were my gracious hosts and sponsors. Professors H. Shelton Smith and Robert E. Cushman of Duke, Professor Franklin Young of the Austin Episcopal Seminary, and my own colleagues, Dean Merrimon Cuninggim and Professor Richey Hogg, have read parts of the original lectures and made helpful suggestions. Mr. Decherd Turner, Librarian of the Bridwell Library at Southern Methodist University, provided indispensable assistance with books and services. Princeton University, with its appointment of me as Visiting Senior Fellow in the Council of the Humanities 1956–57, provided the necessary leisure to finish the book. It goes without saying, however, that none of this host of friends is responsible for the flaws that remain. My final word of gratitude must be to my wife, for inspiration, encouragement, and unfailing help.

A. C. O.

Princeton, N. J.
Christmastide, 1956

CONTENTS

I

ONE

The Ecumenical Fact

FOR those who have any care at all for Christian unity, the ecumenical movement is *the* great representative occurrence in modern Christian history. Within living memory, it has wrought a revolution—in the temper and spirit in which Christians regard one another, in the climate of theological work and church life, in the hopes of reversing the centuries-old drift into division, in the prospect of overcoming the stubborn, self-righteous fragmentation of the people of God. Already, within the past half-century, it has achieved more actual and concrete results in drawing the churches together, in stimulating official conversations and actual unions, in promoting constructive study of the practical and theoretical issues involved in Christian unity—than in the eleven centuries which stretch back from our own to the Photian Schism (867–77).

Most Christians have heard, by now, the story of the great international conferences which stand as landmarks in the first stages of the movement–Edinburgh, 1910; Stockholm, 1925; Lausanne, 1927; Jerusalem, 1929; Oxford and Edinburgh, 1937; Tambaram, 1938; and finally, Amsterdam, 1948. But not enough of us know the saga of the intervening years–of the vision and heroic devotion of the early prophets and giants (men like Mott and Söderblom, Paton and Temple, Brent and Brilioth) and the tremendous achievements of the International Missionary Council, the World Council on Life and Work, and the World Council on Faith and Order.[1]

In our own time and before our very eyes, we have seen first the dream, then the plan and finally the fact of the World Council of Churches. It is *not* a 'superchurch'; it is not the frame of 'the world church' nor 'the cadre of the coming great church'–faintly silly

[1] Three books which, between them, cover this story remarkably well are Wm. Richey Hogg, *Ecumenical Foundations* (New York, Harper, 1952); Wm. Adams Brown, *Toward a United Church* (New York, Scribner, 1946); Ruth Rouse and Stephen Neill, *A History of the Ecumenical Movement 1517–1948* (Philadelphia, Westminster Press, 1954). For an account of recent achievements in church union, see also Stephen Neill, *Towards Church Union 1937–1952*. (London, SCM Press, 1952.) and the periodic 'progress reports' in *The Ecumenical Review*.

phrases that have been applied to it. The World Council of Churches is not even a church at all. It is, rather, a rallying point for the ecumenical movement as a whole—a facility created and supported by its member churches to help them find the ways and means for effective ecumenical study, negotiation, and action.

The Council has a very simple doctrinal formula: 'a fellowship of churches which accepts our Lord Jesus Christ as God and Savior.' Its chief significance is as an earnest of the Christian-will-to-unity, a pledge of obedience to our Lord's command, a mode of reception of God's gift of unity. As long as this will to obedience is present in the churches, as long as Christians are eager to seek and to receive God's gift of unity—so long will the Council be relevant, vital, indispensable. If this will should falter, the Council would falter—and with it, the whole ecumenical enterprise. In this sense, then, the World Council is the token between the churches that they have covenanted together to seek Christian unity according to God's will and by whatever pattern He may lead us to seek and to accept. This covenant has been sharply tested—by the stress of deep-running disagreements and the tensions of high-spirited leaders—and it has been twice affirmed, first at Amsterdam (1948) and then again at Evanston (1954). 'We intend to stay together,' they said, to study and work and worship together—confident that God will lead us onward to the unity which He wills for us.

But if the World Council is the visible focus of the

modern ecumenical movement, its roots and tendrils are in the churches and in the hearts and minds of those Christians in the churches who are deeply discontent and shamed over 'our present unhappy divisions,' those who are seeking the way to true and full community with their fellow Christians. This mood and search has found expression in a network of national, regional, and local patterns of Christian co-operation. The programs of these groups display an almost incredible variety—and do not often emphasize the *theological* perplexities which baffle the ecumenical leaders. They have, however, managed to make commonplace the value and concern for Christian unity. The theologian or church-official who thinks and lives and works *exclusively* within his own denominational orbit and tradition is, nowadays, a faintly odious exception, and not the general rule—and this also begins to be true among the churches who have thus far declined to seek membership in the World Council.

But it is more important to appraise the ecumenical movement than to praise it. For it has come to a critical stage in its development, where its future course cannot be a simple extension of its past. *The ecumenical honeymoon is over*. Looking backward, it seems now that the first great phase of the movement—discovering and charting the major areas of agreement and disagreement —was almost easy (though it seemed far from easy at the time)! Now we are face to face with the residual problems—and they are acute, urgent, and desperately difficult. They are the ancient puzzlers and dividers of the churches: the nature of the church itself and, with this, the proper form of the ministry and the sacraments. Of course, these do not make up the full budget of outstanding ecumenical issues, but they are the chief questions in dispute. Each of them is a matter about which honest and devoted men cannot be careless—and no amount of sentimental yearning will gloss over or bridge the ancient and deep cleavages which they represent.

Moreover, the form of the movement has changed, as in the nature of the case. The early leaders were all devout churchmen, but they often stood somewhat above and beyond the existing consensus of the churches they represented. Now, more than ever before, the churches themselves must be brought along; and the future of the movement begins to depend more and more upon the vigor and vision of the church-leadership (clerical and lay) rather than on the wisdom and diligence of the secretariat of the World Council.

In the great days of 'comparative ecclesiology'—when divided Christians explained their respective positions to each other and discovered how near or how far they stood from one another—it was possible to register significant gains without much radical change being required of the churches themselves. But if we are to reach further agreement about the church, the ministry, and the sacraments, real changes in existing interpretation and practice are required of our divided churches, of our mutually exclusive ministries, and in our doctrines of the sacraments. For as long as devout Christians are conscientiously divided in these matters, the essential aim of common worship and life is tragically frustrated.

The Third World Conference on Faith and Order at Lund (1952) marked an end and a beginning: an end of any hopes that mutual explanations would suffice to overcome division and the beginning of new efforts to overcome the impasse by engaging these hard-core disagreements head-on and in their depths. But this new phase requires a vastly broadened participation in the process of persuasion and change, a greatly heightened sense of responsibility in the churches themselves, a clearer vision of the nature of the unity we seek—and, above all, *a vivid and authentic ecumenical temper, spirit and method in all that we do*. It is about *this* that I wish to speak.

As things now stand, our existing disagreements on the doctrines of church, ministry, and sacraments are 'insoluble.' It would, of course, be no solution at all to press for a 'majority vote,' or to propose a minimal formula from which none could dissent, or to accept as permanent the veto power exercised by churches who insist that their present position is infallible and unalterable. Christian persuasion is the only 'weapon' we have—and all further progress depends on our acknowledgment that, in reality, it is God who 'persuades' us as we seek to be obedient to Him and open one to another. Thus, what matters most is *the atmosphere and temper* in which we propose to live with each other while we go on working with these 'insoluble' problems that confront us.

There are many live dangers which threaten not only the further progress but even the continuation of the movement as an effective force in the life of the churches. If, for example, the banner of 'pure doctrine' is again unfurled as a battle cry by those who claim that their own doctrine is whole and pure, the resulting confusion and acrimony will stifle the will to unity. Or, if those churches that honestly believe they now possess the fullness of the Body of Christ, entire and unblemished, repudiate all the other churches or require submission from them as the price of reconciliation, then arrogance will beget intransigence. Or, again, if the impatience common among 'Free Churchmen' to bypass ancient quarrels and to make a fresh beginning becomes an operating principle, the traditionary churches will, rightly, balk. And, finally, if the depth and stubbornness of our difficulties prompt us to petulance or resignation, so that our present divisions seem more tolerable than the struggle for unity—then we can predict, from a tragic mass of historical precedents, that the ecumenical movement will presently falter and founder. The churches will lose their incentive to stand by the ecumenical covenant, the tremendous achievements of the last half-century will be largely cancelled, and the ecclesiastical bigots and the secular cynics will have their worst prejudices confirmed.

It is, therefore, important to understand why such a woeful disaster is unnecessary—and what hopes we have for active and positive progress. We need to understand *why* the modern ecumenical movement is significantly different from the hundred ecumenical projects in the past three centuries which have started bravely—and failed!

We need to recognize how the modern quest for unity is linked more closely with the Christian sense of history than many of its predecessors—and with a more dynamic view of history, at that. Furthermore, we must consider how it has been providentially led to recover the priority of Christian community over the principle of 'pure doctrine'—and thus has been enabled to make mutual recognition of Christians as Christians the *precondition* of ecumenical work rather than the *goal*. In this perspective, then, we can appraise a third claim: that the ecumenical movement has managed to restore, almost without acknowledgment or conscious intention, the ancient and crucial distinction between *the* Christian tradition which supplies our common Christian history, and the Christian tradition*s* which have often contributed to our divisions and our separate histories as 'churches.'

If men could really grasp the uniqueness of this current ecumenical endeavor, they could then reappraise their deep-dug memories of the myriad failures of past efforts toward the same goal; they could see that what has happened so often before need not happen again. If modern Christians could realize that here, in our own time and open to our own participation, is a movement which has avoided at least some of the basic errors of earlier efforts and bids fair to succeed where they failed, we might then see a new burst of life and power in the movement from that vast throng of church folk who affirm the goal of Christian unity, but who have concluded somewhat sadly that it is not possible in this world, in *our* history.

Christianity has always been plagued by divisions—and Christians have always been striving and hoping for unity. No Christian has ever fully consented to faction, schism, or disunity. And yet all these have happened, and Christians have never been able to live in peace with their fragmented community. Where the breaches were so wide that there was no care for community or where the two communities did not really confess a common Lord, the judgment of heresy could be passed —and anathemas hurled. As long as there was a stable unity and continuity in the great company of Christians, they could tolerate a great deal of diversity-in-unity, for a really catholic church can absorb a great deal of controversial stress and strain.

With the division and decline of the Roman Empire, 'the undivided church' began to drift apart and differences in theological nuances gave rise to harsh and divisive doctrinal controversy. When, still later, in the Reformation, reform and schism came to be almost conjoined, it seemed more natural for the partisans to denounce each other as apostates and heretics than to inquire what it was that Christians still had in common. This reckless polemical spirit did much to make the fact of schism an irreversible affair.

As long as two separated parties recognize that they have some sort of significant common history, a basic common tradition, they are still inside an encompassing community. They may still appeal, in some measure or other, to an authority that is really common to them both. But when their breach is so wide that one party, or both, repudiates their common unity, then immediately the separated groups begin to have separate histories. Often enough, they will insist that their separate histories are wholly continuous with that common history which the separated parties had before. Thus, for example, both Romans and Orthodox still maintain that their respective histories *alone* are really continuous with the common history of 'the undivided church.'

Once schism is an accomplished fact, both parties appeal past the event of schism to the older, common history—unmindful of the fact that the schism itself bars them from a full share in their common history, and so also from any easy prospect of reconciliation. If one party claims that it alone remains intact within and true to the common Christian history, it deceives itself. It then must make 'unconditional surrender' its prime condition to the schismatics for reconciliation with them. If the other party, however, amiably suggests that bygones be bygones, with all differences merged into a warm-hearted jumble, this, too, is a deception—a pretension that history and its consequences can be annulled merely by our wish to have it so.

Divided Christians, in almost every generation since the Reformation—and often before—have sought to come closer to each other, to repair the breaches between them. In this almost constant concern for unity, we may see at least three main patterns and perspectives.

The first, and obvious, thing for Christians to do, if they really feel the pain and guilt of their division, is to dig deep, in co-operative and comparative study, for the residual agreements which they have retained from their common history. These agreements are almost always greater and more important than the controversialists had thought. It is always worth taking a second, or a third, look at a theological controversy—especially one that has resulted in a schism—for one is almost certain to find that the issues were ambiguous in themselves and that they had been disastrously constricted in the heat of doctrinal battle. Polemical theologians have no shining record of being charitable, or even just, to their opponents. Yet even the tyro knows that polemics has bulked very large in the history of Christian theology.

Thus it is always possible that a sympathetic and constructive reconsideration will show that what remains in disagreement does not any longer justify the continuance of the schism. This, for example, was the mood of the Second Council of Lyons (1274)—though not of the generality of the Orthodox, who had been permanently estranged by the inexcusable crime of the Fourth Crusade. Again, it was largely the basis of the Council of Ferrara–Florence (1438–39). From the earliest days of the Reformation there have been Protestants who were deeply concerned for unity—hopeful that disunity could be overcome by comparative study. Melancthon and Bucer strove mightily in this cause, and they have had their descendants who have echoed Peter Meiderlin's famous phrase: 'In essentials, unity; in non-essentials, liberty; in all things, love.'[2] This approach to unity has been also typical of central Anglicanism in every century since the sixteenth.

A second ecumenical pattern, greatly favored by some Protestant dogmaticians—but to be found among Romans and Orthodox as well—is the stipulation of a common authority to which all contending parties must formally submit. For the Protestants, of course, this common authority is the Bible, the sole, sufficient, and perspicuous rule of faith and practice. It was from the

---

[2] For a convincing account of Protestant concern for unity, see John Thomas McNeill's *Unitive Protestantism* (New York, Abingdon Press, 1930); for a short account of Meiderlin's work, see Martin Schmidt's chapter in Rouse and Neill, op. cit. p. 81.

Bible that the Reformers recovered the Gospel—and it was the Bible that served as their only sure bulwark against the Roman traditions and the papal monarchy. But in order to interpret the Bible, the Protestants felt obliged to systematize the Biblical message. It seemed to them self-evident that there is one complete *system* of pure doctrine in the Scriptures—there must be! If this system could only be abstracted and presented, it would afford an authentic platform for the true Christian community. Until agreement is reached on this basis, a Christian convinced of Scriptural truth as it is 'confessed' in his own tradition must not enter into full communion with men who may call themselves Christians, but who read Scripture quite differently (i. e. wrongly). As it turned out, no single system of pure doctrine has ever been extracted from the Scriptures. Men professing to theologize from Scripture, and Scripture alone, came to basic disagreements which could not be further reduced, since they had been derived from ultimate authority. Thus, the Protestants, especially in the first three centuries, were able to maintain their divisions—and multiply them—in defiant good conscience.

A third pattern of ecumenical effort occurred to the Biblical humanists of the sixteenth century—and has continued to appeal to amiable people ever since. Men like Erasmus, Acontius, and George Calixtus saw quickly that the way of the dogmaticians led straight to a stalemate. As a simple and amiable alternative, they sketched out an idealized portrait of the ancient, undivided church and proposed that it serve as a model for the restoration of Christian unity. There was, they stressed, a *consensus quinquesaecularis* (the consensus present during the first five centuries of Christian history) which covered all theological, liturgical, and ethical essentials. If such a consensus were adopted by the contending Christians, it would undercut the fruitless controversies between Rome, Wittenberg, and Geneva. Loyalty to this ancient pattern, they believed, would reduce theological bitterness and increase the chances for reunion. Moreover, it would free the energies of Christians for their proper ethical endeavors in which unity is expressed in practical action.

These well-intentioned ecumenical patterns failed to overcome the tragic separatedness of Christian groups. One obvious reason was that their times were unpropitious. In every case, the cause of Christian unity was complicated by unfavorable political and cultural factors which reduced the freedom of the churches and the theologians to act, or to implement their good intentions. The fortunes of the churches were closely tied to the fortunes of the European states and rulers. A rampant nationalism was itself a divisive influence. The principle of *cuius regio, eius religio* (he who rules determines the religion of his region) meant that the churches could not act apart from the princes and certainly not contrary to their will. These rulers were not invariably opposed to the reunion of the churches—

many of them actually championed the ecumenical cause—but the terms of reunion had to fit the national interests of the respective parties, and these rarely coincided.

But even if the circumstances had been more favorable, the ecumenical patterns we have mentioned have fatal defects in them. The first approach—the method of comparative agreement—works well enough until it reaches the hard core of residual *dis*agreement. Then it tends to generate a brittle mood which all too easily sweeps away the apparent gains. There were fifteen doctrinal issues in contention at the famous Colloquy of Marburg, in 1529. The disputants (Lutherans and Reformed) reached substantial agreement on fourteen of them—but the fifteenth (on the mode of Christ's presence in the Eucharist) was the sticking point, and Luther was moved to dismiss Zwingli and the Strassburgers with the unirenic dictum: 'You have another spirit than ours.'[3] After Marburg, the breach between the Lutheran and Reformed Protestants, hitherto merely threatening—and which Bucer had labored so earnest-

[3] 'Vos habetis alium spiritum quam nos.' Cf. Luther's letter to Jacob Probst, in Walther Koehler, *Die Marburger Religiongesprach*, 1529, p. 130. Leipzig, M. Heinsius Nachfolger Eger & Sievers. Cf. also W. Koehler, *Zwingli und Luther, II*, 141ff. Gütersloh, G. Bertelsmann Verlag, 1953. Cf. also Ernest George Schwiebert, *Luther and his Times* (St. Louis, Concordia Publishing House, 1950), pp. 695–714.

ly to avert—became practically final. Subsequent negotiations were resumed from time to time but they were foredoomed, because of the impossible demand for *total* agreement in *pure* doctrine.

Or again, the appeal to a commonly accepted authority appears logical enough, and hopeful. Actually, though, it has been disconcertingly fruitless. Protestants have a common and deep conviction of the authority of Scripture; this is one of their most constant agreements. An appeal to the Scriptures ought to produce unitive results. In practice, it never has. Consider the Protestant confessions and doctrinal standards, all of which acknowledge the final authority of Scripture and some of which, like the Book of Concord, appeal to *Scripture alone*. An incomplete collection of these confessions and creeds make nearly a thousand pages in Schaff's *Creeds of Christendom* (Vol. III). Each confession is an attempt to state the sum of the essential teaching of the Bible or authoritative guide-lines thereto. The comparison of these confessions has been a major enterprise among Protestant theologians—but they have never proved to be platforms for reunion. Instead, the frustration over their inability to reduce the conflicts between existing confessions has often led theologians to produce yet another. Among the 'sectarians,' the appeal to *sola Scriptura* was also common practice, but turned out to be almost useless in holding or drawing them together. Robert Barclay's *Apology* (the nearest thing to a doctrinal 'confession' that the Quakers produced) is thoroughly laced with Scriptural quotations and references.[4] Yet it failed to commend the Quakers to other Protestant bodies. John Wesley's *Standard Sermons* (still legally normative for Methodists) had, as its sole conscious intent, the exposition of the essentials of Biblical doctrine.[5] The *Sermons* failed to provide a basis for reunion with the Anglicans—or with the Lutherans and Calvinists. The Campbells (Alexander and Thomas) and Barton W. Stone, on the American frontier in the 1830's, were consciously dedicated to the overcoming of the rampant disunity among the Christians around them. Their slogan, 'we speak where the New Testament speaks and are silent where the New Testament is silent,' was intended to be an ecumenical formula. But each of these movements—loyal to Scripture alone, as their adherents sincerely believed—produced new 'denominations.'

For the Bible is always received, read, and interpreted in a community which inevitably compounds its understanding of the Biblical message with its own sense of its 'particular history.' This sense of particular history affects the interpretation of the Scriptures—and uses the Scripture to defend and maintain that particular

---

[4] Robert Barclay, *An Apology for the True Christian Divinity* (Philadelphia, Friend's Book Store, 1877).

[5] Cf. *Wesley's Standard Sermons* edited and annotated by Edward H. Sugden (London, Epworth, 1921). *Preface*, 4, 6.

history. Thus the hope that the Scripture alone can serve as a sufficient basis for ecumenical work miscarries, and the resulting disappointment generates a typical disillusionment which, in turn, becomes defensive and anti-ecumenical. It is not far from this point to the consoling rationalization that disunity is not really a scandal, after all—and may even be compatible with the will of God!

Our third approach to unity—'reconciliation through irenic and practical action based on a minimal creed'—commends itself to moderate men weary of the ordeal and bad humor of polemical theology. For even where it fails, it shields men from the ravages of the *rabies theologorum* (the ragings of the theologians)—of which Melancthon complained, and from which he hoped he would be delivered in heaven! Moreover, there are impressive practical results which have been achieved by Christians who were willing to work together on great and urgent issues, while carefully avoiding doctrinal controversies. But this consentient method fails to envisage the *fullness* of the unity which Christians seek—which is bound to include unity in the whole round of Christian experience: life and work, faith and order, and (above all) unity in sacramental worship. Any simple concession that all church groups which denominate themselves Christians are Christians, comes nearer tolerating the existing divisions than overcoming them. Moreover, this 'Erasmian' approach assumes that as long as the churches are divided the fullness of the

Una Sancta is some sort of future goal still to be gained by further striving in this temper of good will and tolerance. Thus, if the *Una Sancta* is not fully realized in any existing church, it is a sort of far-off, divine event toward which the whole ecumenical effort moves.[6] But surely it is not tolerable for any Christian church which seriously claims the title to agree that full and authentic Christian salvation is not possible and actual, here and now, within itself. In *this* sense, every church does—and must—maintain that its members do truly and *presently* belong to the *Una Sancta*. For even if the churches acknowledge their faults and defaults—and repent of their disunity—still it is this living reality of the *Una Sancta* which makes us *aware* of the sin of division and prompts us to works meet for repentance.

In the providence of God, the modern ecumenical movement has been led by yet another way than any of these toward Christian unity. There are many reasons for this. The first that comes to mind is the tremendous metamorphosis in outlook wrought by the Enlightenment and the nineteenth century. For all its now patent faults, the Enlightenment sought to transcend the vio-

---

[6] Incidentally, this very charge has been laid against the modern ecumenical movement in an interesting and important book by a Roman Catholic who has studied the *literature* of the movement with great care and perceptiveness: Gustave Thiel, *Histoire doctrinale du mouvement oecumenique* (Louvain, 1955); cf. especially p. 173ff.

lent parochialism and insularity which had set European Christians against one another since the Reformation. In science, in arts and letters, and in social issues, the liberal movement generated a sort of ecumenical atmosphere. Even if its main weight was humanistic and even if its utopianism has since been shattered by the shocks of the twentieth century—at least it broke the molds of scholastic Protestantism and accustomed Christians to think in universal terms. Even in our contemporary revolt against the Enlightenment's idolatry of man, we still register its impact in our concern for the *whole* human community —*God's human family*!

A second circumstance favorable to the ecumenical movement was the tremendous chapter in the history of the expansion of Christianity written by the nineteenth century. This 'great Century' (in Latourette's familiar phrase) was distressingly ambivalent. Yet the very success of denominational missions served to expose the anomaly of a divided Christianity trying to carry the Gospel message to every creature. A third favorable factor—of incalculable importance—has been the 'secularization' of European civilization, which weakened the ties between the churches and the civil states, and loosed the churches to act in relation to each other with a comparatively new freedom from political direction and interference. A fourth and obvious factor which has favored new departures in ecumenical action has been the dreadful shock and convulsion of our time, in the face of which the defensive maintenance of separateness on the part of those who claim to have the Gospel for a tragic world has come to seem both pitiful and irrelevant. A fifth item of crucial importance has been the discovery of Eastern Christianity—with its distinctive sense of our common Christian history—by the non-Roman West, and the participation of the Orthodox in the ecumenical enterprise. It is difficult to measure the contribution of Orthodoxy to the making of the ecumenical atmosphere, but it has been immense and will be abiding. Many other factors in our time have gone into the making of a new world—a world in deepest confusion, in constant mortal risk, and yet strangely sensitive to the Christian impulse to vital and authentic community. And all of these have helped to create a setting for a different approach to the age-old problem of unity.

Now, it would be patently wrong to say the modern ecumenical movement has repudiated or discarded the older patterns we have mentioned. They have been retained but, so to say, reoriented in a more comprehensive and truly ecumenical program. We have already seen that, in its first phase especially, the movement was deeply concerned with comparative ecclesiology and the rival claims of the churches. It has sought, constantly and emphatically, for a Biblical foundation in all its work—and has been an important stimulus to the new interest in Biblical theology. Moreover, its record of 'practical Christian action' is genuinely impressive—in some ways its most evident and immediately fruitful success. Still and all, the movement has been led beyond all of these emphases and has been able to include them all in a program which does not rely on them alone.

What makes the present movement significantly different from its predecessors is its prior starting point: the acknowledgment of the *existing* Christian community and the fact of mutual recognition between churches which sincerely 'accept our Lord Jesus Christ as God and Savior.' Modern ecumenism begins with *the present fact of our unity in Christ*, with 'the God-given union of Christ with His Church' (to quote a familiar phrase from 'The Message' of the Lund Conference).[7] This beginning point has allowed the positive recognition, by the separated churches, of the gifts and fruits of the Holy Spirit in the other churches—even when this recognition may include certain reservations as to the fullness and validity of the Spirit's work in those other churches.

The ecumenical movement has made it possible—in a certain sense, has made it necessary—for separated Christians to begin by acknowledging the Christian *koinonia* (community) which already exists among the separated churches, as the essential precondition for ecumenical discussion, worship, and expectation. At

---

[7] The Lund Report, Third World Conference on Faith and Order, held at Lund, August 15–28, 1952, edited by Oliver S. Tomkins (London, SCM Press), 1953, p. 16.

Edinburgh, in 1937, William Temple made the basic point that 'we could not seek union if we did not already possess unity. Those who have nothing in common do not deplore their estrangement.'[8] But if we are willing to recognize this unity that we already have—and to confess that it is not of our own making!—we can then proceed to the ecumenical business in a far different temper than if we approach it with a question in our minds as to whether we can *find* a basis of unity with 'other Christians' *where none now exists.*

To share in the covenant of the World Council of Churches no church has to deny its own validity—although it may be encouraged to recognize and repair some of its own defects. No church has to accept the claims of any other to be the true church—although on closer acquaintance, it may discover and come to cherish the contributions the other churches may make to its own doctrine, worship, and Christian life. Any church in the Council may feel it necessary to deny that the other churches are churches, in the full sense of the term. But no church in the covenant can withhold its recognition of the *vestigia ecclesiae* (the 'vestiges' of the church) in the other churches who uphold the basis of membership and who exemplify the gifts and fruits of the Holy Spirit in their midst. No church can

---

[8] *The Lund Report*, p. 133 (Quoted by W. A. Visser 'T Hooft).

deny to any other *some* share in the common history which we have as Christians.

In this way, the ecumenical movement has re-established the Christian *koinonia* as prior to any agreements about the development of a fully systematized doctrinal consensus. It has rerooted our quest for unity in history —in 'that common history . . . which we have discovered to be longer, larger and richer than any of our separate histories in our divided churches.'[9] It has insisted that the unity we seek be always conceived in maximal rather than minimal terms, but it has warned against any attempt to blueprint our goal or to stipulate the precise path we must follow toward it. It has kept in the very center of all its work the realization that work and prayer for unity must always aim at *the unity God wills for us* rather than the unity we currently will or envisage for ourselves.

In this way, ecumenical Christians have begun by recognizing each other—and themselves—as included in that one community where Christ is Lord and the Holy Spirit is the resident power and wisdom of God—and this as the proper setting for doctrinal debate and the reduction of theological disagreements. *This initial mutual commitment provides the right atmosphere for ecumenical work*. The 'insoluble' issues do not have to be 'solved' by a vote or a showdown. This feeling of

[9] *The Lund Report*, p. 27.

real belonging–of being 'members one of another' in Christ's Body–effectively brakes the inclination to attack and to defense. It helps to dampen the impulse to withdrawal and to recrimination when the going gets rough. Such a program rests its hopes in what God is doing to bring us together and what we may find to do in response and obedience to the divine initiative. This approach readily recognizes that the outcome of our common quest is likely to be quite different from what any one of us would now predict. It is likely to be different from what many of us would now prefer!

We must keep remembering that the ecumenical movement did not begin with the doctrinal issues involved in Christian unity. It began and was a going concern before its leaders thought it even possible to venture into the stormy waters of 'faith and order.' The First World Conference on Faith and Order (at Lausanne) was held in 1927–*after* the International Missionary Council, the World Christian Student Federation, and the Council on Life and Work had already made notable ecumenical gains. Moreover, with the formation of the World Council of Churches (1948), the Conference on Faith and Order was, quite deliberately, reduced to the status of a commission within the Council–and a sub-division of the Study Department, at that. Thus, the present ecumenical program includes, but is not dominated by, the specifically theological issues at the heart of our divisions. This is not a downgrading of the importance of 'pure doctrine.' But it is an effort to set community and doctrine in the right order in relation to one another and to the Christian life.

The World Council of Churches is far from a perfect instrument for the task to which it is dedicated. It has hardly begun to solve the problem of its relations with the leadership of the respective member churches. In an effort to be responsive to the staggering range of need and opportunity before it, it has tended to overextend its resources and personnel, so that many of its projects are being done with more insight than final thoroughness. It is beginning already to take on some of the excess forms of institutionalism and to show the usual sad signs of administrative insensitivity.[10]

Yet, for all of this—despite its full quota of blunders and failures, despite the tendency of ecumenical bureaucrats to know what is best for all of us, and the tendency of denominational bureaucrats to know what is best for the ecumenical bureaucrats, despite the stubborn self-righteousness of those who have the truth and the raucous impatience of those who will not tarry even to ask, 'What *is* truth?'—the ecumenical movement has managed to encompass a vast and motley company of peoples and churches within an orbit that has a single center: the *koinonia* of our Lord Jesus Christ. It has been

---

[10] Yet one must also note an impulse to self-criticism in the WCC not always present in bureaucracies. One of the theological study commissions of Faith and Order has to do with Institutionalism and the WCC is one of its 'experimental subjects'!

enabled to make many separated Christians aware of our unity, *as given us in Jesus Christ.* And this has served to generate in a community which is recovering, as if from a spell of amnesia, the Christian sense of history and our respective shares in it. Such a community has become, for many of us, a veritable means of grace—and can so be for many more!

II

TWO

The Christian Sense of History

When divided Christians recognize one another and seek to move toward each other in common worship, teaching, and life, they are bound to be reminded of the historical nexus that binds them together and links them to the originative Event which was the origin of Christianity itself. They could not acknowledge each other as Christians if they did not have this sense of a common share in the Christian heritage—if they did not see in themselves and the others some kind of continuity with the Christian community down through the ages. This realization of a common history is necessary if we are to make any sense at all out of the claim of our divided churches to belong—in some sense or other—to the one, holy, catholic, and apostolic Church of Jesus Christ.

Lutheranism, as a separate tradition, arose in the second and third decade of the sixteenth century—but many of its sources are in the Middle Ages and in the fountainhead of that medieval heritage, Augustine of Hippo. Anglicanism has a separate history which dates from the Reformation but it also has a common history with medieval catholicism which runs back to first beginnings of the *ecclesia anglicana*. The Methodists have a separate history which begins in the eighteenth century—but still retain ties deeper than sometimes they know with both the English and the Continental Reformers. And back of this reformation and medieval heritage lies the history of the patristic church, in which all of us have as much of a share as we are prepared to claim. All this means that none of us knows even the separate history of his own particular church really well if that is *all* the church history he really knows or cares about.

But it means more than that. One of the most important discoveries in ecumenical work is that when men with separate church histories make conscious, sympathetic efforts to re-enter and understand church histories other than their own, they are almost always drawn closer to each other.[1] The more catholic and compre-

---

[1] Cf. Oliver S. Tomkins (ed.), *The Third World Conference on Faith and Order, Lund, 1952*. (London SCM Press, 1953), p. 27. See also my article 'A Way Forward from Lund' in *The Ecumenical Review*, (Vol. V, No. 1, October 1952), pp. 59–63.

hensive one's historical understanding and concern, the less polemical is his conception of the uses of historical knowledge. There is a common Christian history—and the more clearly we perceive it the more positively we are prepared to push beyond existing separations as neither final nor irreconcilable.

For the Christian who is content with his own separate history and disposed to minimize any linkage with the entire Christian past, there are two main options, both involving an appeal past history to immediate authority. One choice is to leap-frog history and turn directly to the New Testament, as the touchstone of faith and the model of the contemporary church. Since the Word of God speaks in and through the New Testament as nowhere else, we can safely ignore the years that intervene between us and the New Testament, save as they aid in this primary task of hearing and obeying the Word. From this standpoint, the long ordeal of the church in its struggle to clarify and fill out the New Testament message appears as mostly irrelevant or actually misleading. The Bible is directly available to men in every new age; it is this common access to its truth which constitutes the true bond of unity among Christians at any given time—and if they hear the Word in faithful agreement, they are indeed one. In this direct approach to the revealed Word of God, history is foreshortened, judged, and, in a certain sense, disposed of.[2]

Yet there is a subtle self-deception involved in this anti-historical approach. The Biblicist is usually unaware of the extent to which he has already been conditioned, one way or another, by the history he now chooses to ignore. The result is that his interpretations of Scripture follow a pattern strangely similar to certain already existing hermeneutical traditions and at odds with others. The history of Biblical interpretation shows us many fascinating parallels between the patterns of Biblical theology and historical theology—nor can we find any instance of a Biblical theology not conditioned by the historical background and circumstances of the interpreter. Give a basic New Testament passage to an Orthodox, a Lutheran, a Calvinist, an Anglican, and a Congregationalist to interpret—and the discrepancies in their interpretations will correlate much too closely with the various historically conditioned traditions in which they stand to justify any claim that they did no more than reproduce the original meaning.

Another choice, if history is to be ignored, is to appeal to the authority of immediate Christian experience—the point of meeting between God and man here and now. If God's Holy Spirit *is* present with us *now*, the faithful believer has open access to God's will and purpose for his life, whether or not he knows much of the Christian past. Devout prayer, group exercises in the devo-

---

[2] Cf. Heinrich Emil Brunner, *The Misunderstanding of the Church* (Philadelphia, Westminster Press, 1953), as an example of some such view as this.

tional life, the Spirit-born impulses to witness and to love, the 'mountain-top experiences' which inspire and transform men—these are the significant signs of the Spirit and they suffice to assure men of 'the witness of the Spirit' and to draw 'like-minded' men together. This is the typical emphasis of pietism and illuminism.[3] It, too, is anti-historical, for the only elements in Christian history that interest the pietist are the examples which he can find there of 'religious experience' in other ages. But pietism is doubly deceptive. On the one hand, its final measure of the validity of religious experience is religious experience! Thus, when pietists disagree on really serious points, their normal recourse is *separation.* On the other hand, they do produce a great deal of history—chiefly tendentious and separatist—chiefly in the form of biography of their own spiritual heroes. In either case, pietism and illuminism, for all their concern about unity in the Spirit, have contributed a good deal less to the ecumenical movement than their unitive professions might imply. The chief reason for this, I suggest, is their stress on 'inwardness,' which readily becomes a sort of spiritual self-centeredness—the surest sign of a lack of the sense of common history.

Simply to talk intelligently to one another, churchmen in the ecumenical movement have had to widen

---

[3] Cf. Elton Trueblood, *The Essence of Spiritual Religion* (New York, Harper, 1936).

their scope of historical knowledge and to revise a great many of their preconceptions and misconceptions of the historical experience of other communions. To be sure, much of this historical study has been primarily apologetic—the Protestants against the Romans, Protestants against other Protestants, with the whole lot of us engaged in the almost new experience of getting acquainted with the history, and *the sense of history*, of the Orthodox Church. But the unintended and imperceptible results of historical study—when conducted in the ecumenical spirit—are the lifting up and highlighting of the common heritage shared by the separated churches and the raising anew of the problem of the integrity and the continuity of the Christian community, in all its diversity, in space and time.

The recognition of a common Christian history must not blur the historian's perception of the pluralism and manifoldness of Christian history. He must beware of the trap into which Gottfried Arnold fell,[4] of mingling the history of heterodoxy and orthodoxy in a sort of mystical jumble. Yet we might also remember that Arnold's concern to understand doctrinal aberrations from a careful and positive analysis of the sources, rather

[4] In his *Unparteyische Kirchen-und Ketzerhistorie* (1699-1700), in which Arnold, a pietist and a mystic, undertakes the first sympathetic and 'fairminded' study of the literature and history of the medieval and Protestant 'sects.'

than merely from the charges of opponents, went far toward liberating church history from its dogmatic blinders. In any case, the historian must keep asking himself what the divided fragments of Christendom have had *in common?* What is it that warrants the use of the adjective *Christian* by groups with separate institutional histories?

Our common Christian history is not merely the sum of our separate histories and certainly not their lowest common denominator. Rather, it is the sense which all Christians have that God has acted in *our* history and that *this* history is the medium of His revelation. It thus includes the conviction that the history which separates us from the Event of Christ is also the indispensable nexus which *connects* us with that Event—and thus connects us with each other. That is, I take it, what Father Georges Florovsky means by his phrase 'ecumenism in time as well as in space.'[5]

This Christian sense of history, implicitly stimulated by the ecumenical movement, needs to be made much more explicit. It needs application to our present condition, in which many of us are somewhat smugly content with our own partisan histories (or our parochial conceptions of church history) and are slightly conde-

---

[5] First used in a sermon in the Lund Cathedral, in a worship service of The Third World Conference on Faith and Order, August 1952.

scending toward other partisan histories as far as we have troubled to study them. To overcome this, we must come to recognize the common history which we have as separated Christians—in whatever measure or degree we can claim that it truly belongs to us.

Christianity is a historical religion. This means more than that Christianity is a historical phenomenon, that it *has* a history. It means that everything in the Christian message roots in a unique historical event, which gathers up the old history of the people of Israel and creates the new history of the Christian community. The Christian gospel inescapably has to do with events in time, in and through which God has revealed Himself—and in such a fashion that the revelation can never be abstracted from its historical context. In short, we believe that God has chosen to reveal Himself in genuinely concrete events—and to appoint the procession of concrete events (history) as the bond between the events of revelation and *every subsequent event*. The Christian community emerged as the effect of such a revelatory event (the Event of Jesus Christ, that act of God's *self*-revelation which sums up *all* revelation). It has continued to this present moment by means of the historical process of receiving, renewing, and transmitting the essential encounter of that first community. Christians of today, in all our separated communions, are dependent upon the infinitely complex process of transmission by which this apostolic witness has reached us—and on the integrity of the process which links us to the originative Event of Christianity.

Every Christian has a Christian history. It is the sum of all the past events accessible to his memory and judgment, which have served to re-present to him the apostolic witness to Jesus Christ. It is the impact of the Christian past upon the Christian present which confronts men with the claim of Jesus Christ to be the living center of their existence. It was in some sort of historical community that each of us heard the Gospel *preached*—and at a time when we could not judge whether it was preached well or ill. Then, as we discovered the *past* of our own communion, and the past of other and disparate communions, we began to have some fuller measure of the common meaning of the Gospel we have heard and believed and the Gospel as believed and practiced by others.

In this respect, the discovery of our total Christian past is the means of fuller initiation into the whole Christian family. Man is a creature capable of inheriting acquired characteristics—not through his genes but through his traditions. Children are knit into family life by hearing the reminiscences of the family. It is the sense of *this particular family's tradition* that makes its 'members' truly kin, since the blood relation in itself is not sufficient to produce the feeling of true belonging. So, from age to age, the Christian community has told its story—'of Jesus and His love,' to put it in the phrase of a gospel hymn—in many different versions and with a baffling variety of church forms to contain it. Yet, at its heart, the story had a valid center: 'that Christ died for our sins according to the Scriptures, that he was buried, that he was raised on the third day in accordance with the Scriptures.' etc. (1 Cor. 15:3ff). This echo of the earliest *kerygma* (apostolic preaching) contains within it all the essentials of God's *traditum* (handing over) of Jesus Christ 'for us men and our salvation.' Paul received this part of the *kerygma*, probably from the Jerusalemite church, and he handed it over (*tradidit*), '*as of the very first importance*,' to his Gentile hearers. And this same process of hearing, believing, and transmitting the essential reality of the Christ-Event has been the principal business of the Church throughout its history. The originative Event must not be 'rescued' from its historical setting—not even to save it for the 'eyes of faith.' And the historical linkage of the evangelical tradition *through time* cannot be ignored—not even to give us some 'better way' of direct access to the Event through the Spirit.

Christianity is fixed to a 'point' in time—to the strange, literally marvelous, events of the birth, career, death, resurrection, and triumph of Jesus Christ, and the new age and community of God's Holy Spirit which He ushered in. No man can become a Christian save as he is brought back to these originative events and re-enters them, with both historical imagination *and* responsive faith. Historical knowledge and imagination avail naught without faith. On the other hand, Christian faith is literally unintelligible without the *propaideusis* (preparation) of historical imagination and insight. If we are to believe and proclaim the Gospel of the Christ-Event, we are forced to a concern about the *historical events within the Christ-Event*, as well as the revelatory and redemptive meanings of that Event.

Modern Christians are increasingly aware of the critical difficulties involved in any effort to re-enter the events which surround and support the Christ-Event, by means of critical analysis and historical imagination. Historical critics have raised sharp—and proper!—questions about the precision and reliability of the historical evidence that we have for reliable knowledge of the life and ministry of Jesus. In reaction to historical skepticism, many modern theologians have come very near to agreeing that the historical details of Jesus' life and ministry do not really matter since the only crucial question is the decision or response of faith which Jesus Christ and the *kerygma* call us to make.

But there is a deep and sure instinct in good Christian preaching through the ages to 'tell the story of Jesus,' to recall the essential events which delineate his life and teaching and personality—as we can make them out from a careful study of the deposit of apostolic testimony. To be sure, the testimony of the witnesses varies; the testimony underwent important changes during its oral transmission; not all of the details are accurate and many details which would seem important to us have been omitted. But the essential details are there. The data which delineate Jesus' character and career are established—and this on grounds which are adequate for any historian whose skepticism is not derived from motives other than historiographical caution. And, if this is *not* so, then not even the Christ-Event can be rescued for faith.

If it were demonstrable that the essential form of testimony about Jesus in the early church is wholly unreliable, if it can be shown that what we claim to know of the events *before* Easter and Pentecost cannot be significantly correlated with the events of Easter and Pentecost—then the honest conclusion would have to be drawn that Easter and Pentecost were *theophanies*, that the originative Event of Christianity is not really historical after all. In this case, Christianity would have to stand among the mystery cults (with their symbolic stories of gods who 'lived' and 'died' and 'rose again'), or among the wisdom cults (like that of Apollonius of Tyana)—or become a religious philosophy (which is essentially what Bultmann proposes it to be).

Christians have, therefore, a vital stake in the course of the historical criticism of the New Testament, for it involves the peril of our losing the full Gospel of '*this* Jesus' (Acts 2:22-26; 3:12-26; 7:55ff; 10:34-43; Hebrews 5:7; I Peter 1:11). And yet it also holds out to us the promise of making good our basic claim of the Gospel that God's self-revelation was in *our* human time, in *our* human history, that *our* high priest is 'one who in every respect has been tempted as we are, yet without sinning,' who is, therefore, 'the mediator of a new covenant' (Hebrews 4:15; 9:15).

No one has ever contended that historical-critical knowledge of Jesus of Nazareth amounts to full and saving Christian faith—not even the liberals who set such a store by their hope of an adequate 'life of Jesus.'[6] Many men knew Jesus 'in the days of his flesh'—and the vast majority did no more than note that he was 'one of the prophets' (Mt. 16:15). Our historical knowledge, even if it were far better than it is, is nothing more than a preparation, a means of encounter with the reality of 'this Jesus whom God has made to be both Lord and Christ.' But it is also nothing less. Without it, the full mystery of 'the man Christ Jesus' is not encountered and faith cannot respond to the fullness of God's redemptive deed in Him. No man rightly believes the Easter story unless he has, so to say, gone *behind* the Easter-event

---

[6] Cf. Albert Schweitzer's 'classic' study of this epoch in New Testament criticism in *The Quest of the Historical Jesus* (3rd ed., London, A. & C. Black, 1954). And for a sample of the confusion in New Testament theology on the issue of Christian faith and primitive Christian history, see the collection of essays in the controversy over Bultmann's proposal to 'demythologize' the New Testament in *Keryma und Mythos*, edited by Hans Werner Bartsch (Hamburg, Reich-Evangelischer Verlag), 5 volumes. The first volume has been translated into English by R. H. Fuller as *Keryma and Myth* (London, S. P. C. K., 1953).

and has re-entered and experienced something of the pre-Easter fellowship of the disciples with Jesus. Otherwise, his Easter-faith is nothing more than faith in the Easter-faith of the early church—and he has still not *encountered Jesus Christ*, whose earthly life was the meaning-giving preface to his death and resurrection. Moreover, he is bound to a tale of his fathers which can never be brought to the judgment-bar of history, and which has, therefore, become a tradition without a measure. On the other hand, if his Easter-faith is only a poetic or mythical way of pointing to a universal truth about God and man, for which the *idea* of Jesus as the Christ serves as a symbol (exempt from the need of any real historical correspondence), he has exchanged the *concrete* mystery of the New Testament for an *abstract* mystery of religious philosophy—a drastic alteration of the very terms of Christian faith.

Christianity, therefore, stands or falls by its claim that its originative Event is historical, that this Event illuminates all other historical events, that this Event is known and 'reproduced' in the ongoing life of an actual historical community. Undercut any one of these and you have shattered the foundations. The fact that they have weathered the storms of unbelief and the persistent buffetings of heresy from the very beginning through an unbelievably complicated history gives some proof of how fast and firm they stand.

From this common possession of a Gospel in and for human history and existence, there has arisen a Christian sense of history—which sees the Event of Jesus Christ *and* the continuing life of the Christian community as indissolubly bound together in a process in time which is both historical and providential. History is the story of God's actions in His world in calling together and building up a covenant-community ('the people and household of God'). History is the story of that community in its preparation, its origination, and in its long, confused pilgrimage toward its God-given goal.

For the Christian, then, history is not the transient flow of time through static forms and institutions (as for the ancient Egyptians). It is not the interplay of natural laws of balance and equilibrium in human affairs and the nemesis which brings down those who disrupt this balance (as in Herodotus). It is not an affair of chance, either, or of fortune (as in Thucydides and Polybius). History is not cyclical (as for the Stoics) nor the unfolding of some ideal structure of being (as in Vico and Hegel). Finally, it is not a fully managed puppet show, with God the puppeteer.

When we say that God is in history, it does not mean that He is a prisoner of process, nor that human freedom is annulled or overridden. God is the source and the judge of all historical process rather than the *immediate cause* of historical events. He assigns to them their meaning and place in the out-working of His purposes, which are as unvarying as the means may vary. Thus history is an affair both of process (*chronos*) and of decision (*kairos*). Its events share all the relativity and finitude of all other items in the causal order. But there are *some* events, no less processive than the rest, which thrust crises upon men—force them to exercise their freedom, lift them above the flow of time, and call them to act *in* the living NOW, as free creatures of a free Creator. The historical events recounted in the gospels, as history, are of this order. Thus the Christian must judge them in two aspects. He must make a historical judgment about them—knowing that all historical judgments are relative, problematical, and finite. But he must also respond to them existentially—seeking their meaning in God's meaning for history and seeking also to hear God's Word for him in his own life. Thus, he seeks both to hear the Word of God in and through human words, and to obey it, in and through faith.

But if history is the struggle for authentic community of men with God and one another—and the resistance and struggle of unfaith and ill-will against this divine purpose[7]—then the Christian must realize that both 'sacred' and 'profane' history are of equal moment to

---

[7] This is the central gist of Augustine's conception of history as the struggle between the two *civitates* (commonwealths): one, the *civitas terrena* (commonwealth of earth) and the *civitas Dei* (God's commonwealth). In the first, community, such as it is, is achieved through the centripetal force of *self-love*. In the 'city of God,' the unifying power of community is *love of God*—the ruler of *both* cities and of *all* history. See R. H. Barrow, *Introduction to Saint Augustine* (London,

him, if he is to respond aright to God's word. The great climactic Event in history which gives to all other historical events their proper meaning is the center of our faith. But, no less so, the vast complexity and continuity of events which enrich and confirm our understanding of the central Event belong to the substance of our faith as well. In this perspective on history, the cleavage between 'sacred' and 'secular' is overcome by the sense of the integrity of history within the providence of God.

The Christian sense of history amounts to one's awareness of *his own share* in the total history of the whole Christian community—centering in the Christ-Event and continuing through all the ages as the essential medium-of-witness to that Event. To know the relations of our own churches to Jesus Christ, we must know of Christ's presence and activity in His Church in every age and through all times. Only thus can we mark the line between the diversity of gifts and forms allowable in the church and the corruption of truth and grace which fractures Christian community.

The Christian, then, is perforce a church historian—in some degree or other. The better historian he is, the more sensitive he can be to the defects and needs in his

---

Faber and Faber, 1950), p. 161ff. See also *De Civitate Dei*, XIX, 17, 25-8, and Etienne Gilson's introduction to Demetrius B. Zema and Gerald G. Walsh's translation of *The City of God* in *The Fathers of the Church* (New York, Fathers of the Church, 1950), Vol, I, pp. xi-xcviii.

own inheritance—without drawing the false conclusion that this inheritance must be repudiated forthwith. The better his sense of Christian history, the more readily he can understand and appreciate the values in traditions other than his own—without supposing that they can be simply added to his own. He can be more discriminating in his distinctions between 'essentials' and 'non-essentials.' Most of all, he has a sense of history's true orientation—its grain and goal and destiny. History is a mystery, but one in which men in the living present can come face to face with the Lord of all history and recognize the true identity of Him who 'was and is and is to be.' From this they can pass to a true identification of themselves, of each other—and of their common lot.

The course of history is a drama of judgment, suspense, and hope. In it we must recognize man's fight against God, which leads him into conflict with himself and his fellows. We must acknowledge that, all too often, those who have called Jesus 'Lord, Lord' in the most confident, orthodox, and graceful tones have not been really concerned to do the will of our Heavenly Father. We must admit that, in sloth and caution, in 'righteous' zeal and anger, in betrayal and division, we ourselves have not only followed Him afar off, but have led others astray. And yet the drama moves on and God's unwearying patience and costing love still abounds toward the children He has called and is redeeming. Christ's church is just that company of the called and redeemed as they have moved along the pilgrim way toward the 'end' of history, to the consummation of God's purpose in Jesus Christ's *parousia.*[8]

This is why our sense of history and our sense of community are so deeply linked. When either suffers, the other suffers with it. When amnesia comes upon a generation of Christians, when they are unmindful of who they *were*, or what they have as their rightful legacy from the total Christian past, it is all too easy to concentrate on who they are now and to magnify the distance between themselves and other Christians. What is more, their common ground of interpersonal relationship is sharply constricted, as it would be between *two* victims of amnesia. Both the unity and vitality of Christianity depend upon a common memory, a common hope—and a common faith rooted in that memory. Thus, the historicity of the originative Event, the continuity of witness to that Event and its current meaning are all equally crucial to vital Christian faith and fellowship. And this is why Christianity cannot long survive as an abstraction, religious or ethical; why its effectiveness is tragically reduced by its fragmentation into confessional groups and parties—each with an inerrant Book, or an infallible Pope, or a self-validating 'experience.' Every abstraction of Christianity—whether toward speculative heresy or static orthodoxy, or even in

---

[8] Cf. Edmund Schlink's address to the Lund Conference, 'The Pilgrim People of God,' in *3rd World Conference on Faith and Order*, pp. 151–61.

a self-centered isolation!—is essentially anti-historical and fatal to the genius of historical Christianity.

And yet, for all our insistence on our linkage through history with the concrete realities of the Christ-Event and the life of the Christian community, we must also take notice of the other side of this same truth. Historical Christianity—the church visible and militant in the earth, with all its grievous faults and shortcomings—is authentic Christianity and the vital medium of the Gospel through the centuries. There is no other way to identify Christianity than by its *total* history! *But*—and it is a sizable 'but'—the historic Christianity of any given past age can never be simply reproduced in any living present. In this sense, the Christian past is *really* past—and even the most faithful imitation of any earlier Christian period, in imitative form, language, and ethos, produces an inevitable archaism.

This is what we mean by the term 'archaic,' is it not: the maintenance of past forms that have lost their living spirit? And this points up the paradox of a historical religion. A religion which is essentially different from the basic guide-lines of historical Christianity would simply not be authentic Christianity. And yet a mere continuation or reproduction of historical Christianity is not vital Christianity either.

For vital, authentic faith arises when our sense of history is touched and transformed by our sense of God's present action at the living edge of our own history. History supplies us with the data of believing—and this is prerequisite—but faith itself comes from God's transformation of our historical knowledge into personal decision and involvement.[9] History shows us God's *traditum* (His gift of love and grace in Jesus Christ)—and illuminates to us the process of its transmission in and through the ages. But there must be yet another movement, an *actus tradendi* (an act of handing over), by which God 'hands over' the wondrous gift to *us*, in our day and situations, so that we, too, may become *contemporary disciples*! In and of itself, even the liveliest historical imagination does not suffice to transform 'the there and then' (*illic et tunc*) into 'the here and now' (*hic et nunc*). This is why historical judgments are inescapably problematic judgments. Certitude and true contemporaneity of Christian faith cannot arise until Jesus Christ (of the there and then) meets us in living encounter in the here and now. And this is the work of the Holy Spirit. Thus we can say that the Christian sense of history must always include a sense of the mystery of the interaction between the really past and the really present—and so acknowledge that history is the arena of the action of God's Holy Spirit.

When I say this, I can well imagine a good historian's

---

[9] Cf. H. Richard Niebuhr, *The Meaning of Revelation* (New York, Macmillan, 1941)—a modern theological 'classic' which turns around this very point.

wincing—for to talk about history, mystery, and the Holy Spirit all in one breath may seem to 'modern men' to compound fuzziness. But this only goes to show how far we have let the illuminists carry us in their separation of the process of history (gross, causal, entropic) from the work of the Spirit (immediate, vital, free). And yet, for historical Christianity, the plainest meaning of the Holy Spirit's 'office' is: God at work in the living present revealing to us the meaning of the Christian past, centered as it is in God's Self-revelation in Jesus Christ. In this representation, the Spirit gives meaning to *that* revelation in the life of the church *today*. The work of the Holy Spirit is to bring men up-to-date: to make them contemporary witnesses; to transform Christian history into personal faith. It is the Spirit who performs the *actus tradendi*, and so makes Christ our contemporary. This was Jesus' promise of the Paraclete: 'When the Paraclete comes, whom I shall send to you from the Father, even the Spirit of truth, who proceeds from the Father, *He will bear witness to me* (John 15:26) . . . He will glorify me, for He will take what is mine and declare it to you' (16:14—but see also 14:16-19; 14:25-29; 15:26–16:1; 16:7–15). And the stretching out of history's time-span, far beyond any expectation in the early church, has not reduced the power of the Spirit to make faith spring forth from the soil of Christian memory. The *medium* of the Holy Spirit's action is—*history!*

Pentecost was the birthday of the Church. The disciples had been with Jesus and so had shared in the history that framed the Passion and Resurrection. But it was not until the coming of the Spirit in full reality that they knew who they were and the meaning of what they had witnessed. And once this had happened, they were able to witness to God's act in Christ and to proclaim a Gospel of repentance and new life. (Acts 1:8). *This* was the church—the community of witnesses to Jesus Christ and man's salvation wrought by him. But the power that makes the church, that continues it in time, that renews its faith, in each new historical epoch, even as history changes its forms—this is the Holy Spirit: God's real presence and action in the church, and through the church, 'in all the world.'

To be a Christian is to have come to know Jesus Christ in this historical community which has been enabled, by the Spirit's power, to be His witness in all the world. It is to share in the church's power to witness, in life and word and deed, in the community and to the world around. Faith arises and grows in a living community, aware of its traditions and open to the vital action of the Spirit. We enter such a community by receiving its tradition and traditions—as the boy Jesus did, seeking out his Father's Temple, 'sitting among the teachers, *listening* to them and *asking* them questions' (Luke 2:46).

Every man comes to Christ on the testimony of other witnesses to Christ and to His saving power. He professes his faith before such witnesses, in common with the church's profession of faith. His faith is a double indication that he has believed the witnesses, on the one hand, and also that he is in genuine encounter with the living Christ to whom they witnessed. His faith in the witnesses (i.e. the church) is never the same as saving faith itself, for that is born only in response to our hearing and heeding God's Word in Christ. But his faith in the witnesses is the prerequisite to saving faith. And this prerequisite faith comes to us through the church in history. Moreover, it is verified in and through the church's history. This is why a deep and comprehensive understanding of the church's history tends toward a recognition of the God-given unity of the church. For there is the center of our common Christian history—Jesus Christ in His church, remembered, witnessed, interpreted, preached, and worshiped. This center of the church's history recalls all faith to its historical rootage, its historical continuity, its participation in common history—and so fuses the preparation for hearing the Gospel, the Gospel itself, and its faithful hearing into one integral experience in the living present.

By some such way as this, then, we come to claim our share in the Christian tradition and to discover a central thread of identity and continuity in that tradition which runs through the tangled web of our separate and partisan histories. To be a Christian at all is to be aware of the Spirit's work of bringing Christ to us and bringing us closer to each other in the fellowship of His grace. To recognize others as Christians, in spite of the differences in their partisan histories from our own, is to acknowledge in them this same mysterious work of the Spirit—uniting history and faith. This mutual recognition lifts a man or a denomination above partisan history, by just so much as they are able to see God's will to draw us all together in a faith and a unity which will fulfill our common history. It is of the essence of the ecumenical vision that we see not only the past reality but the future promise of God's unswerving design to make of His children 'a chosen race, a royal priesthood, a holy nation, God's own people.' And the purpose of this design is that there should be a truly catholic community 'to declare the wonderful deeds of him who called [us] out of darkness into his marvelous light' (1 Peter 2:9-10).

Thus our common history—the history of the witness of faithful men to God's redemptive love in Jesus Christ—stands over against our partisan histories and separate traditions. It rebukes those who are content with their separate histories and those who claim that in their *separate* histories the *whole* of the common history may be found.

Partisan history cannot aid in the restoration of broken community. Nor yet can we pass from our present 'unhappy divisions' to the unity which God wills for us, until we recognize this wider orbit of Christian community in which we are set by baptism and faith and the deeper continuity of the Christian tradition in our presently divided confessions. When men know that they are one in Jesus Christ, they know, too, that it is this relation which holds them together in community, which is the prerequisite of unity in all things else. It is this experience—this possibility of mutually sincere profession of faith in the one Lord Jesus Christ on the part of Christian groups who differ widely in many basic concerns—that the ecumenical movement offers us as a live option. And from this knowledge of our common Lord and our common history of confessing Him as Lord there comes then the realization of the unity that we have even now. But more, it also gives us the grounds for hope that its fullness may yet become manifest among us.

The ecumenical movement in our time has provided a fellowship of churches in which Christians with diverse and separate histories might discover and acknowledge the common share of other Christians in that one *koinonia*, in which Jesus Christ is truly Lord and the Holy Spirit constantly resident. This experience of mutual recognition of Christians by Christians has, of course, been unsymmetrical and incomplete. Not all of the participant churches are prepared to admit that all the others are equally authentic churches or have equally valid ministries and sacraments. The pain of separation affects some traditions quite differently than it does others. The residual tensions of the movement are still as urgent and have become even more acute now than they were ten years ago. They scarcely promise to abate in the next decade.

And yet, for all this, despite painful head-knockings over doctrine, despite heart-rending separations at the Lord's table, despite the distance which divides us in ecclesiology and churchmanship—the covenant of the World Council of Churches still holds firm: 'We intend to stay together!' And this intention marks the reality of the Christian community, the continuing influence of our common Christian history. It is also a sign of the veritable action of God's Holy Spirit in our midst and in our history.

Let us try to look ahead a generation. What would happen if, during that time, a significant number of Christians in all the denominations began to recover from their general amnesia and indifference toward the Christian past? Suppose that a steadily increasing company of Christians caught the vision of ecumenical study and co-operation, and so began to care more and more to seek unity—together? Suppose that a new generation of pastors and teachers arose in the churches who had a vivid sense of our common history as a Christian community through the ages. Suppose that many Christians, across many barriers, were taking the trouble to share in the experience of common worship, work, and study with other Christians—thus widening their horizons both in space and time? Suppose there were many more church leaders—bishops, moderators, presidents, theologians—who were really disposed to recognize the gifts and fruits of the Holy Spirit, *wherever found*, and to celebrate such gifts and fruits as tokens of that unity we are seeking?

Would there not then be a good hope that such a generation would begin to outgrow separate histories and present divisions? Would it not then be possible to reclassify our presently 'insoluble' problems as at least 'probably soluble'? Might we not confidently expect imperceptible and unpredictable changes that would dissolve present rigid barriers? And would this not be the leading of God's Spirit toward the goal *ut unum omnes sint* (that they all may be one), an earnest of which we already have?

This leading, this growth, has already begun. The experience of a great host of men, high and low, who have lived in the atmosphere of the ecumenical movement testifies that this is so. The effect of these gracious and inspiring experiences furnishes the ground for an honest faith and hope that what has already developed will continue to unfold. In such a process and atmosphere, more and more Christians will discover this common history which we have had all along. More and more Christians would recognize *the* essential Christian tradition among all our separate traditions. More and more Christians would find positive answers to the present harsh dilemmas in faith and order.

This is the hope and the promise of the future—that we shall see in history, and in our own ecumenical fellowship, the real presence of God's Spirit, who has been and is still leading us into the truth as it is in Christ Jesus. And if we are willing to be led, this same Spirit will bring us together and build us up into the household of God—the one, holy, catholic, and apostolic church of Jesus Christ.

III

THREE

The Christian Event and the Christian Community

We have tried to suggest that the Christian sense of history amounts to a sense of the Christian community, created in time by the Event of Jesus Christ and persisting through time as witness to Jesus Christ by the power of the Holy Spirit. The history of this community has been checkered and diverse—baffling in its complexity and ambiguity. But that it exists at all, and can be recognized by modern Christians, is because of their common response to Jesus Christ, from whom the community derives its distinctive reality.

One of the unique aspects of the modern ecumenical movement is that it has made this sense of community the prime basis of its fellowship and work. It has thus recovered the 'right' order of relationship between the sense of Christian community and doctrinal consensus in the community—taking doctrine here in a sense large enough to include polity and liturgy. The recovery of this 'right relationship' is one of the most distinctive and constructive achievements of the movement and goes far to explain its 'success'—thus far! We must, therefore, look more closely into this relation between community and doctrine—to see what is still required of us if the movement is to continue in its forward motion.

The thesis I would like to suggest—even though time and space forbid its full elaboration—is something like this: *Christian community is primary; Christian doctrines are explicative.* A doctrinal system, a developed liturgy, a settled polity, all these are achievements possible only *within* a community that has its life and power from another originating source than these. And when community is lost or fragmented, unity cannot be achieved by even the most strenuous efforts to reestablish doctrinal consensus (as prerequisite to restored community). Instead, the quest for unity between the divided Christians must begin with the mutual recognition of their actual community in Jesus Christ. For it is only in *the atmosphere of acknowledged community* that the quest for doctrinal consensus has any lively hope of succeeding. Our work in Faith and Order has immense importance in clarifying and confirming the ecumenical reality. But it does not create it.

The essential reality in the Christian life is participation in God's deed in Jesus Christ which generated the original Christian community. But how can *this* be real—

for men living in an age far removed from the originative Event? For, in one basic sense at least, this Event is now another among the events of human history. It is *past*—and can be recovered for a later time only by the exercise of historical imagination and judgment. Thus, the historical-critical analysis of the entire range of Christian history is a vital necessity for the renewal of the sense of community. But it is never sufficient in and of itself. For one thing, the historian, as such, can never quite explain why such an event should have produced such a community—or how it has managed to maintain its identity through succeeding generations and epochs. For another, *quâ* historian, he can never explain the interior reality of saving grace.

Simply as a historical event, the ministry of Jesus Christ did not create the Christian community. This is why the simple historical inspection of that event does not re-create or restore unity among divided Christians. Only as the Christian past is re-lived and re-newed by an experience of living faith in Jesus Christ, here and now, does the reality of Christian community dawn upon us. And, as we have seen,[1] this is the work of the Holy Spirit, who brings to each new Christian—in each new generation—something of *his own Pentecost*. Assent to the message of the Christian community is not, in itself, living and saving faith. But faith is based, in

---

[1] Cf. Chapter Two, p. 56ff.

part, upon assent to witnesses. It requires a historical preamble!

The emphasis upon historical preambles is an interesting feature of early Christian preaching. In Peter's 'sermon' at Caesarea, he begins with an appeal to 'the story of Jesus'–assuming that even his Gentile hearers knew its main outlines. 'You know . . . ,' he says, and then goes on to interpret the saving import of the historical event (Acts 10:34–48). Paul reminds the Corinthians that, in his first preaching, he had passed on to them the most precious memory of the Church–in the form in which it had been preserved from its earliest origin. There is good evidence that the Eucharistic pericope in I Corinthians 11:23–26 is not Pauline in origin or even in form. Joachim Jeremias has convincingly shown that 'Paul was handing on that formula of the words of institution which was in use in Antioch where he had settled about A. D. 40.'[2] The basic text (derived from a comparative analysis of I Corinthians 11:23–26, Mark 14:22–26, Matthew 26:26–29, Luke 22:17-19) 'is identical with the text of Mark.'[3] Thus, in Paul and Mark, we have two independent reports coming from different sections of the church which agree

---

[2] J. Jeremias, *The Eucharistic Words of Jesus* (Oxford, Blackwell, 1955), p. 131. Cf. ibid. pp. 103, 108.

[3] Jeremias, op. cit. p. 115. Cf. the elaborate footnotes on pp. 115–16, with citations and bibliographical references.

even on the wording of the original institution pericope.

The import of this is that at the heart of the Christian Eucharist, itself the heart of Christian worship—and developed before any written Scripture—there was from the beginning a conscious act of memory which was linked to the words and deeds of Jesus himself. This memory runs back of Easter and Pentecost. It contains both the sum of Jesus' historical career and the foretaste of the eschatological Kingdom. The Eucharist is, therefore, *the Christian memorial par excellence*, because in it the historical preface and the new miracle of Christ's living presence in the Supper are fused. But the Eucharist is also more than a memorial, for in his full sacramental reality Jesus Christ is really and truly present, here and now. It is a sacrament in which a historical memory has been imbedded as an essential ingredient.

By the time of the Epistle to the Hebrews, the church stands at least a half-century away from its point of origin. One of the epistle's aims is to magnify and interpret the universal and eternal priesthood of Jesus Christ. Yet of all the New Testament writings, save the Gospels themselves, Hebrews is most concerned with the historical preface to faith. It might almost be regarded as a fifth Gospel! Moreover, it was in this same general period, after the destruction of Jerusalem and the dispersal of the Jerusalemite church, that the Gospels were produced—to ensure the possibility, in any future time, of the proper fusion of faith's historical preface and faith itself, the possibility of getting *back of* Easter and Pentecost in order to come *toward* them properly!

The emphasis on historical recall appears in the shaping of the Christian tradition in the ante-Nicene church. Ignatius of Antioch gives it emphatic stress.

'Stop your ears [he commands the Trallian Christians] when anyone begins to talk to you apart from the actuality of Jesus Christ, David's scion and Mary's son, who was *actually* (ἀληθῶς) born, who *actually* ate and drank, who *actually* suffered under Pontius Pilate, who was *actually* crucified, who *actually* died while heaven, earth and the nether-world stood by gaping; who *actually* rose from the dead—resurrected by His Father, who will also resurrect us who believe in Him through Jesus Christ.' [4]

This concern about the historical preamble to the Gospel is really a concern about the Christian community and its origin. The community is the product of this *total* Event, and not just the apostolic doctrine about this event. It is the fruit of God's self-manifestation in history and not just an *idea* of God-in-man. Thus the way into the community is not, in the first instance, by way of doctrinal understanding—but rather through encounter with Jesus Christ, as He is remembered, proclaimed, and interpreted by the community and its tradition. The

[4] *Epistle to the Trallians*, IX.

heart of Christian faith and the living center of the Christian community are one and the same, the Lord Jesus Christ. Church doctrines emerge and take shape as a function of this community. They represent the church's effort to comprehend the inexhaustible importance of the Event to which everything in its faith and life is related. Thus the stress upon the historical preamble to faith and the historical continuity of the community of faith become chief elements in the church's struggle to maintain the Christian message and to guard it against heretical distortion.[5]

Christian preaching must always appeal, in some fashion or other, to the apostolic preaching.[6] This preaching laid the historical footings of the faith firmly because they tie the Gospel of repentance and faith to the apostolic community—to its origin and to its continuity in time. In that first community, the human reality of Jesus Christ was taken for granted. For subsequent generations, it must be attested to by the historical data of the apostolic preaching and the New Testament. Take this away, and the church has no grounds for its confession

---

[5] Cf. H. E. W. Turner, *The Pattern of Christian Truth* (London, A. R. Mowbray, 1954), especially chapter VIII.

[6] For a generally accepted analysis and summary of this, cf. C. H. Dodd, *The Apostolic Preaching and Its Developments* (London, Hodder & Stoughton, 1936), and R. H. Strachan, 'The Gospel in the New Testament' in *The Interpreters Bible,* Vol. VII.

that our Savior was of 'the very same essence as ourselves in respect of his humanity' (Definition of Chalcedon.) We know precious little about these historical data but that little is very precious—for on it depends our ability to be able to retain the New Testament clarity about our Lord's *humanity*. Any neglect of the historical preamble to faith looks in the direction of monophysitism (exclusive stress on the divine 'nature' of Jesus Christ). It has been no accident that when Christians began to concentrate on the technical niceties of the Christological dogma—inescapable and crucial as they are—they became mostly concerned to secure the full and real divinity of Jesus Christ. And even though orthodox Christology, in both East and West, has always confessed our Lord's humanity (the really controversial point in the Chalcedonian 'definition'), it has actually shown a strong tendency to minimize or to neglect its full import for Christian faith, worship, and life.

To hear the Gospel, then, men must attend to the witnesses of the great Gospel events *and to the succession of these witnesses in the church*. But, equally, the good news of Easter and Pentecost must come afresh to every Christian and it must bring us something of the same induement of faith, inspiration and power which enables us to witness in our turn. This re-newal of the Christian Event is the heart of the Christian community and the center of such unity as we have—in baptism and Eucharist, in doctrine and teaching, in common history. One's first hearing of 'the story of Jesus' may—and usually does—leave a person uncomprehending and un-understanding. This is certainly true of children; it is almost equally true of adults. The tendency, then, is to accept the faith of *the preacher*, if he appears to comprehend the inner import of his message—and to live his message. But this is never enough. As Augustine put it, we must also go through the same stages by which Peter came to faith—in order to share Peter's own faith: 'Not that we should believe in Peter, but in Him whom Peter believed . . . so that Christ himself, who was Peter's master in the teaching that leads to life eternal, becomes our Master, too.'[7]

The Christian community was constituted by this complex and mysterious Event: the life, teaching, death, and resurrection of Jesus Christ—and the swift following consequences of Pentecost and the rise of the new community. The sign of the Christian is his faith in Jesus Christ; his tie with every other Christian is their common confession. For 'he who confesses the Son has the Father' (I John 2:23)—and this confession is possible only by the Spirit. 'By this you know the Spirit of God: every spirit which confesses that Jesus Christ has come in the flesh is of God' (I John 4:2).

It goes without saying that the Christian community did not arise in a conceptual vacuum. The minds of the first Christians were firmly shaped by their Jewish doc-

---

[7] *City of God*, XVIII, 54.

trinal heritage—and its re-interpretation to them by Jesus himself. Even the bare bones of the apostolic preaching have doctrinal substance, and the profoundest doctrinal implications. The themes and issues of all Christian theology are germinally contained in the confession that 'Jesus Christ is Lord, to the glory of God the Father.' But the full dogmatic explication of this pre-dogmatic confession had to be developed as an ordeal of reflection and debate within the community which made the confession.

Theology arose as a servant *of* the community. This was, of course, an inevitable and proper development, for the church could not simply *repeat* its message in later ages and in different contexts. The theological enterprise went on within the continuing community and its evolution makes an astonishing story. On the one hand, the history of early Christian doctrine shows a desperately unstable process, full of confusion and divagation. Many of its pages make painful and disillusioning reading. On the other hand, it was amazingly stable in its essence and outcome—and the proof of this is in the fundamental identity of the various creeds and rules of faith, the various ecumenical formularies, and the major 'systems' of doctrine.

The doctrinal equipment of the ancient Christian community was disconcertingly meager and motley. 'Heresy' sprang up along with 'orthodoxy.' Indeed, 'orthodoxy' was called out by the need to safeguard the *kerygma* from distorted interpretations of it. Theological experimentation was rife in the ancient church. Moreover, it inevitably involved novel interpretations of the Christ-Event. Every change in the doctrines of the person and work of Jesus Christ involved a consequent change in the pattern of life in the Christian community—for the two are so closely interrelated that a shift in either affects the other. The organization of the church was elementary. The expansion of Christianity into new areas and dimensions of the Graeco-Roman world created an unending series of crises and difficulties for the church. Yet the community of Christians was maintained with amazing steadiness and confidence—in the teeth of persecution and through successive periods of demoralization in the community. For the Christians knew what had brought them together and what held them together. And in this knowledge they could work at the business of doctrine and liturgy, with the *traditum* of the Gospel as their datum-plane and the *actus tradendi* of the Spirit as their motive force.

Two basic tendencies in the doctrinal development in the ancient church are worth our notice in understanding the relation between the community and its doctrine. The first is what we might call *the rule of protreptic instruction.* The great bulk of the Christian literature of the period is occasional and deliberately unsystematic. It deals with actual concrete issues confronting living men—but by striking them obliquely so that they might learn *for themselves* what they needed to know to maintain and enrich their imperfect understanding of the Christian life. The prevalent form of Christian teaching is catechetical. The aim is *to involve the reader in the process of understanding* rather than to confront him with a developed system of doctrine. The fact is worth pondering that Origen's *On First Principles* (*c.* A.D. 220) and John of Damascus' *On the Orthodox Faith* (*c.* A.D. 745) are the only two deliberately systematic doctrinal systems in the first eight centuries of the church's history.[8]

The other widespread feature is what we might call *the rule of minimal doctrinal development*. Christian thinkers had to respond to the need of doctrinal clarification and to the challenge of heretical interpretation. But there was among them a general resistance to large or unprecedented speculative forays. It took the church more than three centuries to hammer out the final form of its trinitarian dogma (I Constantinople, A.D. 381) and another three centuries thereafter to determine the basic requirements of an authentic Christology (Chalcedon, A.D. 451; II Constantinople, 553, and III Constantinople, 680-81). And this whole process was accomplished

---

[8] The typically proptreptic method in ancient theology may be seen, in all its diversity, in the antiheretical writings of Irenaeus and Tertullian, the *Proptreticus* of Clement of Alexandria, the *Catechism* of Cyril of Jerusalem, and the *De Catechezandis Rudibus* and *Enchiridion* of Augustine. Another main feature of all this literature is its *exegetical character*. Even Origen was far more the Scriptural exegete and commentator than he was a 'systematic theologian.'

amidst very painful conflict and theological chaos. But we must note at every point the obvious reluctance of Christians, at any given point, to venture much beyond the bare minimum of 'progress' in new terminology or new conceptions. The process was essentially *conservative*. The prevailing interest of each of the ecumenical councils was to maintain the Christian tradition as it had been received from the Christian past. Even in the case of a first rate speculative genius like Origen, he carefully binds his speculation to the church's rule of faith and sincerely intends to be 'a man of the church.'[9]

The Christian community has been living with inbuilt doctrinal confusions during its entire history. And yet it has also shown itself capable of absorbing violent shocks and of entertaining great doctrinal diversity—so long as the common Christian witness and teaching remains essentially faithful to the originative Event and in continuity with the apostolic community.

Even from so brief a summary as this, I hope that we can see the meaning of the thesis that Christian community is the *prius* of Christian doctrinal construction and consensus. Sound doctrine is an undeclinable responsibility of the Christian community—but this responsibility can be discharged only within the community which knows itself constituted by the Christ-Event. Theology serves the church in explication of its own reality, in

---

[9] Cf. my article, 'Origen and the *Regulae Fidei*' in *Church History*, VIII, No. 3, pp. 212–21.

interpretation of the Gospel to others, and in defense of the Gospel against distortion, whether in doctrine or practice. The Christian community lives by its Spirit-bestowed power to receive, renew, and transmit the Gospel. Age after age, it can do this because of the reality and continuity of the community in which doctrinal reflection can know its proper source and aim.

The church's response to the ordeal of heresy is instructive.[10] The first thing to note is that it seems never to have occurred to the church that it might deal with all conceivable heresy in advance or, so to say, once-for-all![11] It took on the heresies as they arose: now

---

10 There are several recent books on this subject of great importance: S. L. Greenslade, *Heresy and Schism in the Early Church* (London, SCM Press, 1953—New York, Harper, 1953); H. E. W. Turner, op. cit.; Ellen Flesseman-Van Leer, *Scripture and Tradition in the Early Church* (Assen, Van Gorcum, 1954); J. N. D. Kelly, *Early Christian Creeds* (London, Longmans, 1950); R. V. Sellers, *The Council of Chalcedon* (London, S. P. C. K., 1953). Older books of considerable importance are G. L. Prestige, *Fathers and Heretics* (London, S. P. C. K., 1940) and Damien Van den Eynde, *Les Normes de L'enseignement chrétien dans les trois Premières Siècles,* Universitas Catholica Lovaniensis, Series II, Tomus 25, Paris, Gemblaux, 1933.

11 Tertullian's *De Praescriptione Hereticorum* is not an exception to this generalization. He did believe that the rule of faith was competent to deal with any heresy but he himself applies it only to issues which confront him—in this case the claim of Marcion and the Gnostics that the Scriptures were *their* authorities, too.

docetism, now ebionism, now Marcion, now the Gnostics, now the Montanists. The Christian concern with heresy was the threat it posed to the identity of the apostolic tradition and to the continuity of the Christian community as the bearer of this tradition through history. For heresy is not primarily a matter of doctrinal aberration (although this is always involved). At bottom, heresy is contempt for the Christian community and its particular center of faith and life and its peculiar role in the transmission of the Gospel. The vast majority of the heresies are Christological—denials of the full reality of the Incarnation in either its human or divine aspect. They undercut either the historical preface to Christian faith or its ecclesiological consequences. Even in Montanism—whose followers professed the creed and rule of faith—we see a false disjunction between history and revelation.

At the heart of heresy is the claim that 'true Christianity' or 'true religion' is *something essentially different from historical Christianity*. Thus, heresy disrupts the continuity of the Christian community, and 'breeds off the line.' Its end-product is a *different kind of community*, with a different center of authority and a different bond of fellowship. Orthodoxy, in its best and proper sense, is care for the Christian community. It is the understanding of what brought the community into being, what holds it in being, what thrusts it forward through history.

The problems which beset the conservers of the

Christian tradition are well illustrated in the Arian controversy. It was difficult, at first, for the generality of Christians to recognize any mortal threat from the Arians, for they made the usual basic confession of Jesus Christ as Son of God as Lord and Savior and offered him worship.[12] It was only at Nicea, when the Arians produced a creed which made plain their aberrant interpretation of this profession, that the majority of bishops could see the issue. Theodoret tells us that they were so upset by their belated discovery that they tore the Arian creed to shreds amid angry cries.[13] Thereafter, in the long, complicated struggle, it is interesting to see that whenever the Arian tenets were clearly stated–and their import clearly grasped–the Christian mind recoiled from them. Despite the vicissitudes of the church in the half-century after Nicea, it was never in serious danger of becoming Arian.

But the 'orthodox' Christians could not deal with the brilliant dialectic of the Arians by appealing to Scripture and the existing tradition. By ingenious interpretation, the Arians could carry their appeal to the same authorities. It was found necessary to add terms and distinctions to the current creeds which were neither

---

12 Cf. J. F. Bethune-Baker, *An Introduction to the Early History of Christian Doctrine* (London, Methuen, 1949), p. 165ff.

13 Theodoret, *Church History*, I, vii.

Biblical nor traditional (e.g. *homoousios*). These additions became stones of stumbling to common Christians, especially in the East, who were deeply attached to the conservative principle.[14] The Nicene position triumphed only as the Christian East was persuaded—and it took fifty years!—that the new developments were actually more faithful to the original tradition than some of the intervening developments in Christian thought (e.g. Origenism) to which the Arians had appealed.

But the main point for us is that in this long, messy business the Christian community held steady and firm because it enjoyed a *given inner unity* which was never deeply shaken. That which had brought it into being still sustained it and guided its basic inner life. This sense of *internal organic integrity* was its strongest bond of unity. Even in the disorders of the theological disputations, it was this integral linkage with the whole history of the church which was the chief preservative against drastic disintegration.

I suggest, then, that what preserved the Christian community in its first five centuries was this firm, clear sense of the right order of relations in the Christian community. Its origin was the Christ-Event, its organ was the church, the deposit of its message was the Scripture.

---

[14] Cf. the letter of Eusebius of Caesarea to the Christians of his diocese in which he defends himself against their criticism of having gone beyond tradition—Socrates, *Church History* I, viii.

The measure of sound interpretation was the rule of faith and the Apostolic symbol. The clarification of this message came in developed doctrinal constructions and the precipitate of all this process appears in the ecumenical creeds and dogmas. This 'right order' could sustain a great deal of tension and inner diversity.

But internal organic integrity in the community began to dissolve as the world into which Christianity came began to fall apart. With the West in the death-agony of an old civilization and the birth-throes of a new one, and with Byzantium increasingly an arthritic civilization under siege, the two halves of the church drifted in opposite directions and the channels of communication between them slowly clogged up. The strange affair of the Photian schism (867–77) illustrated the difficulties which the two divided segments of the Christian community were having in their efforts to maintain their common history.[15] But this sense of common history, though severely disrupted more than once, was never really blotted out—not even by the excommunication of Michael Caerularius, Patriarch of Constantinople, by Pope Leo IX, in 1054. This is commonly cited as the date of the final rupture between East and West. Actually, it was only a very severe crisis in the long

---

[15] Cf. Francis Dvornik, *The Photian Schism* (Cambridge, Harvard Press, 1948) for a brilliant reconstruction of the incident and a demonstration of how Baronius supplied Western historians with a false image of the entire affair.

drawn-out process of alienation. Pope Leo's bull was not confirmed by the Roman curia; the other Eastern patriarchs declined to join Michael in his counter-blasts at the Pope. The doctrinal substance of Catholicism and Orthodoxy remained practically identical. Their liturgies, though quite different, were never a serious bone of contention—not even the Filioque, which has sometimes since been magnified to appear as if it were the main issue. Actually, isolation from each other plus new and alien developments in each half of the Christian community atrophied the *sense of community* between them—and when this deterioration had gone far enough, their essential doctrinal consensus was helpless to hold them together.

The decisive end of all significant community between the Orthodox East and the Roman West came with the Crusades. The Fourth Crusade, launched ostensibly to liberate Jerusalem, turned into a massive raid on Constantinople instead (1204). The spectacle of Western Christians burning, looting, and raping in the capital of Eastern Christianity was profoundly shocking even in a barbarous age. [16] The Catholic effort to set up a 'Latin Empire of Constantinople' weakened the Byzantine community beyond effective recovery and marked

---

[16] Cf. Steven Runciman, *A History of the Crusades* (Cambridge, Cambridge Press, 1954), Vol. III: 'There was never a greater crime against humanity than the 4th Crusade' (p. 130).

an end to all real community between East and West.

The ephemeral Latin Empire of Constantinople came to an inglorious end in 1261; but the hatred of all things western, for which the Crusaders were responsible, long survived its fall, and is still one of the psychological factors which make difficult any rapprochement between the East and the West. Seen from the East, the permanent embitterment of the relations between Christians and Moslems and between Eastern and Western Christians appears as the main fruit of those Crusades, which from another angle may be considered as part of the spiritual renaissance of Western Europe.[17]

Even after their sense of community was shattered, the Western and Eastern churches continued to make sporadic overtures toward reunion. The Second Council of Lyons (1274) reached a formula of agreement, but it was an empty gesture. The East was too embittered to accept it. Something of the same thing followed the Council of Ferrara-Florence (1438–39), where a sort of formal agreement was reached which was thereafter repudiated. Thus two separate histories sprang up—each equally positive that it was *the* common Christian history. Orthodoxy, for many centuries, made out of its enforced isolation a dogmatic principle, and now is only slowly re-entering the forum of ecumenical discussion

---

[17] Rouse and Neill, op. cit. p. 17.

and life. Rome went on from the schism to the development of a papal monarchy and the production of novel dogmas which have multiplied the difficulties of reunion.[18]

Within itself, Orthodoxy has continued to maintain the primacy of community in the Holy Spirit—and thus has kept to the ancient order of Event-Community-Doctrine. This has made possible a more flexible conception of unity and a greater diversity in doctrine and polity. It underlies the development in Orthodoxy of the several autocephalous churches, all in communion with the Ecumenical Patriarchate—but not under its direct control. It has provided the basis for the Orthodox doctrine of the Christian fellowship in the Spirit which embraces even schismatics—and all baptized Christians—in the wide orbit of Christian charity and grace. This has allowed Orthodox theologians to participate in ecumenical work with other Christians whom they cannot regard as full members of the true church—and this in a very different spirit from that of the Roman church. Nevertheless, Eastern Christianity has been deeply isolated from the rest of the on-going world—and it has transformed its conviction that the church

---

[18] Nevertheless, one of the effects of the ecumenical movement has been to stimulate new interest in the relations between Romans and Orthodox. Cf. the important symposium *L'Église et les églises* (Chevretogne, Editions Chevretogne, 1955).

is perpetually inspired and guarded by the Holy Spirit into the claim that the church itself is thereby infallible and inerrant. From this it follows that the entirety of Orthodox traditions are infallible and the church is irreformable.[19] This position is bound to cause serious difficulties for Protestants, who are equally clear that one of the marks of the church militant is its being *semper reformanda* (always being reformed).

It is difficult to say when or how Western Christianity came to exalt the primacy of pure doctrine and to insist upon a single infallible *magisterium* (teaching authority) *in* the church. Latin Christianity shows strong practical, legalistic tendencies even from its beginnings. Doctrinal conformity came easier in the West. Rome was rarely hospitable to speculative flights or diversity. During the conciliar period, while the East was in a prolonged uproar, Rome continued to insist on its relatively simple formulas (derived largely from Tertullian, Ambrose, and Hilary) with regard to the doctrines of the Trinity and the Person of Christ. The victory of Leo's *Tome* at Chalcedon—crucial as it was—was more of a triumph of an established doctrine than a strengthening of the sense of community between divided Christians. Rome has tended always to confuse community with conformity.

---

[19] Cf. Hamilcar Alivasatos, 'The Holy Greek Orthodox Church' in Newton Flew (ed.), *The Nature of the Church* (New York, Harper, 1952), pp. 41–53.

Then, when the terrible burden of a disintegrating society fell upon the Western church, there was an urgent need to be able to define the truth and to administer the corporate life in accordance with a visible measure of truth. In a welter of secular communities, the church sought to extend the Christian community by exalting its *magisterium* and using its sacramental power as a mode of discipline. In the turmoil of the 'Dark Ages' the church was almost swallowed up in the maelstrom of feudalism and came near to losing both its freedom and its unity. The papal monarchy which emerged from this struggle with the secular powers was more than an administrative office for preserving the supra-national character of the Christian community. It was also a means of *locating* the visible *magisterium*—the source of pure doctrine by which true community is achieved or maintained.[20]

The dogma of papal infallibility (Vatican Council, 1870) is a rigorously consequential development of this conception of a visible and located *magisterium*. Where conflicting views arise affecting faith and morals, there must be a single determinant of propositional truth—if

---

[20] Cf. Boniface VIII, *Unam Sanctam;* see also Philip Hughes, *A History of the Church* (London, Sheed and Ward, 1947-48), III, p. 56–101. Cf. Walter J. Burghardt, 'The Catholic Conception of Tradition in the Light of Modern Theological Thought' in the Catholic Theological Society of America, *Proceedings of the Sixth Annual Convention*, June 25–27, 1951, pp. 42–75.

we are to preserve a community constituted by pure doctrine. History cannot settle such matters, nor even Scripture and the church-as-community. There must be a single and final resort–and God has thoughtfully provided the Roman church with it. The *Pontifex Romanus* is the *supreme* judge of all the faithful. There is no authority greater than the Apostolic See–and no man may lawfully appeal beyond its judgment (*iudicium a nemine fore retractandum*). No one has the authority to pass judgment on the judgment of the Bishop of Rome (*neque cuiquam de eius licere iudicare iudicio*).[21] When the Roman pontiff speaks *ex cathedra*, he cannot err. Moreover, his definitions do not require the consent of the church; they are infallible and irreformable in and of themselves.[22] To be in the Christian community means to be in communion with the Roman bishop. With its new dogmas–and with recent papal encyclicals that have the intentional force of incontrovertible decisions–the modern papacy has fully explicated the claim of Pius IX: 'Tradition? *I* am tradition.'[23]

The German and Swiss revolts against Rome were urgent protests against the pretensions of an unreformed

---

[21] *Decreta dogmatica concilii Vaticani de fide Catholica et de ecclesia Christi*, ch. III. Cf. Philip Schaff, *The Creeds of Christendom* (New York, Harper, 1882), II, pp. 262–6.

[22] Ibid. c. IV.

[23] Cf. Walter Burghardt, S. J., op. cit. p. 75.

papacy in the firm control of an unreformed church. The Reformers were not careless of the Christian community, but they were deeply certain that the Roman church was no longer the community in which Jesus Christ was the vital center. Martin Luther's recovery of the Gospel, focused as it was in the meaning of faith, was achieved *before* he found it necessary to break with Rome. In the beginning of his revolt and in the early debates with the Roman emissaries, Luther readily appealed to church history, to the councils, to the *consensus communis fidelium* (the agreement of the community of the faithful). This recourse to the Christian past was an honest expression of his own deeply conservative tendencies. Yet these appeals failed. None was infallible, and he believed, even as the papists had, that there must be a single infallible authority which could settle all disputes. Thus, he turned to Scripture as the sole guarantee of the Gospel of salvation by faith alone. And then he found that he had to tear the Scriptures out of the hands of those who maintained that only the Roman church could interpret them infallibly.

A better case can be made out that the French and Swiss Reformers began with a rediscovery of the Scriptures and were led by less dramatic stages to the *sola fide* (justification by faith alone). Yet even Zwingli—and certainly the younger Calvin—conceived of Scripture as the *medium* in which they heard the living Word of God. Their initial sense of community was strong and their initial concern for unity was deep. It is remarkable how widely the Reformers agreed on a formal definition of the church: 'a congregation (community) of faithful men wherein the Word of God is purely (*recte*) preached and the sacraments duly (*recte*) administered.'[24] In original intent, this was an *ecumenical* formula—but the stone of stumbling was, of course, in those adverbs, 'purely' and 'rightly.' In the disputes which arose—and in the absence of a powerful ecumenical *atmosphere*—the Reformation moved from its original stress on the Scriptures as the *topos* (place) where the Word of God speaks to men, to the notion of the Scripture as itself the Word of God, verbally infallible. The *sola fide* comes finally to depend on the *sola Scriptura*.

One of the tragedies of the Reformation was that its appeal to Scripture alone left no appeal beyond it. This yielded irreducible and acrimonious disagreements. There is no doubt that the vast majority of the Protestant leaders were aiming at the restoration of the

---

[24] The Augsburg Confessions, Art. VIII (Schaff, op. cit., III, pp. 12–13). Cf. The Scotch Confession of Faith, Art. V and XVI (ibid. III, pp. 442–3; 458–9); The Savoy Declaration, 1658 (ibid. III, pp. 721–9); The First Helvetic Confession, A. D. 1536, XV (ibid. III, 218–19); The Second Helvetic Confession, XVII (ibid. III, 271–7); The 39 Articles of the Church of England, XIX (ibid. III, 499); Irish Articles of Religion, 1615 (ibid. III, pp. 538–9); Westminster Confession of Faith, 1647, XXV (ibid. III, pp. 657–9); New Hampshire Baptist Confession, 1833 (ibid. III, pp. 746–7); Confession of the Free Will Baptists, 1834, 1868, XV (ibid. III. p. 755); Methodist Articles of Religion, XIII (ibid. III, p. 810).

Christian community. They were not tolerant men, but they set no premium on faction itself. They were not intent on rule or ruin. There was a constant and sincere unitive urge among them.[25] It was a matter of deep frustration to them that their unitive principle of *sola Scriptura* did not produce that restored community which they desired. Its failure to do so left them hopelessly divided—and worse yet, left them divided in considerable good conscience and self-righteousness.

To implement its appeal to Scriptural authority, each major Protestant group felt itself impelled to formulate a definitive and systematic interpretation of the Biblical message. Thus arose the Protestant confessions, catechisms, articles, standards of doctrine, and the like.[26] Each of these is bound to the Scripture and intends to say nothing more or different than what the Scriptures say. Yet in their practical outcome, they came to be an appeal *beyond* Scripture—to serve as a vantage point from which the Scriptures could be rightly viewed and understood. The irony of this procedure becomes terribly poignant when these confessions, each based on a common authority, fail to agree among themselves.

Thus it turned out that the Protestant effort to reduce disagreement actually hardened it. One of the many reasons why so many Protestants came finally to de-

[25] Cf. John T. McNeill, *Unitive Protestantism* (New York, Abingdon, 1930).

[26] Cf. Schaff, op. cit. Vol. III.

spair of a united church–and occasionally even to sanctify disunity by holding it to be the will of God!–is surely this: the bitter choice forced on them between a false community (the Roman church) and the impossibility of true community according to their own principles.

Thus it came natural to them to place pure doctrine (*reine Lehre*) above visible community.[27] Pure doctrine–and by this they meant the *total system* of Christian doctrine–is the prerequisite to restored community. Until this can be achieved, divided Christians do better to possess the Biblical truth (as they believed they had it!) in fractured community than to grant or receive communion on any other terms.

By the end of the seventeenth century, the principle of divided Christendom had become firmly established. It had been case-hardened in the horrors of the Thirty Years' War (1618-48), it had been rationalized by a triumphant Protestant scholasticism, and it had been compounded by the well-nigh universal consensus that intolerance is a theological virtue. The dogmaticians kept kneading and turning the Scriptures in stubborn

[27] Cf. R. Seeberg, *History of Doctrines* (Grand Rapids, Baker Book House, 1952), II, pp. 363–426–especially Seeberg's rueful preface to this section: 'The great prophetic age of Protestantism was followed by a didactic age. We can understand the necessity for the transition; but it proved a retrogression similar to that from the days of the old prophets of Israel to the Great Synagogue!' (pp. 363–4).

confidence that they would eventually yield a unitive doctrine. Princes kept turning and kneading the churches in the impatient demand for conformity and civil obedience. And the early voices of the Enlightenment epoch were beginning to say that orthodox Christianity is incurably bigoted, divisive, pitilessly intolerant–inimical to human progress and well-being.[28]

The sects, dissenters, and pietists, all sought to keep alive the vitality of the Gospel and the obedience of the Christian life. Persecuted themselves, they usually held no hope of a reunited Christendom. Indeed, the only sort of Christendom that they knew seemed committed to a ruthless determination to stifle the free spirit and to identify community and conformity, much as the Romans did. It was natural, therefore, that the only sort of unity they cared about was the *koinonia* of the spiritually kin–and this was possible whether the dominant

---

[28] Cf. Pierre Bayle, *Dictionnaire* (3rd. ed.), II, 1533. 'Christianity (of the 16th and 17th centuries)' [he says] is a sanguinary, murderous religion, which had been hardened to the shedding of blood for some five or six centuries past. It had contracted a very long-ingrained habit of maintaining itself and of seeking aggrandizement, by putting to the sword anything that offered to resist it. Faggots, executioners, the frightful tribunal of the Inquisition, the Crusades, the papal bulls inciting subjects to rebel, seditious preachers, assassination of princes—these were the regular means that this sixteenth (and seventeenth) century Christianity employed against those who would not submit.' Cf. also John Locke, *A Letter Concerning Toleration* (1689).

church was a whole or a heap.[29] they sought for tolerance and they nourished the evangelical spirit—but they offered no really constructive solutions to the problems of the nature of the church, its ministry and sacraments. The residues of pietism and nonconformity are an important part of the ecumenical heritage, but are not very productive for these 'insoluble' issues which are currently so critical.

The nineteenth century turned much of the classical Protestant pattern upside down. In the name of tolerance, humanity, and reason, it sought to overthrow the authority of both church and Scripture. In the name of scientific history, the Biblical revelation was domesticated in the history of religions and put to the service of a universal morality. Liberal Protestantism—the baptized offspring of the Enlightenment—came to promote Christian fellowship wholeheartedly but, typically, with never more than a halfhearted interest in the problems of church, ministry, and sacraments. It did much to revive a concern for history and something of the Christian sense of history. But its prevailing notion of ecumenicity was generally indifferent to the deep issues that had divided the Christian community. Furthermore, its indifferent ecclesiology tended actually to pro-

---

[29] Cf. the literature of English Non-Conformity—e.g. Robert Browne, *Reform without Tarrying for Any*, Richard Baxter's *The Saints' Everlasting Rest*; John Wesley's 'The Catholic Spirit' in *The Standard Sermons*, XXXIV.

voke the conservatives and 'high-churchmen' to intransigent reaction. An interesting example of this was the Oxford Movement. One of the lessons to be learned from nineteenth-century Christianity, therefore, is that care for community without a corresponding care for apostolic doctrine is as one-sided as its Scholastic opposite.

The ecumenical movement of the twentieth century has sought to profit by the lessons of the past. It has restored the right order of Christian Event–Christian community–Christian doctrine. It has laid the main stress on the God-given unity already real in the divided churches. It arose, as we know, in a series of almost informal common projects in discussion, work, and worship—in which Christians *began* with mutual recognition of each other as Christians and with a common witness to their common Lord and common history. As the movement gathered momentum and shape, a basic working agreement developed among ecumenical Christians that *they would do nothing separately that they could conscientiously do together*. The leaders of the movement, from its earliest stages, were widely diverse in their ecclesiology, but they were clear in their conviction that it is the unity of the *Church of Jesus Christ* that was their aim and goal.

The ecumenical task, as they saw it, is to move from the initial perception of our God-given unity in Christ to a fulfillment of this unity in the church. In this way, the ecumenical movement has recovered the patristic principles of *maximal community* and *minimal doctrinal consensus—as a starting point*! Instead of trying to produce a 'confession' to which all could subscribe—which, in the actual circumstance, would have been a lowest common denominator—the ecumenical movement accepts, at face value, the reality of Christian fellowship among those who 'acknowledge our Lord Jesus Christ as God and Savior.' This fellowship, once recognized, makes the further quest for the fullness of unity possible and hopeful.

The results—certainly to one who has surveyed the sorry history of the strife of Christians through the centuries—have been surprisingly gratifying. In the ecumenical atmosphere, differences have been candidly exposed and disagreements plumbed in their depths. But the disposition to break off, or else to impose solutions by some sort of coercion, has been checked by the undeniable reality of the community that has encompassed the antagonists. The story of the early ecumenical conferences (Stockholm, Lausanne, Jerusalem, Edinburgh) makes moving reading. It is still inspiring to remember the excitement that came with the surging sense of discovery of the reality of the Christian community. And even now that the movement has produced an enormous mound of literature, this motif is still one of the most basic. The fact that Christians can act together (and worship, too) in good faith and mutual recognition has become the means of yet deeper penetration into the common history and faith which is the fullness of what we have already comprehended, in part.

This communal spirit survived the tempests of two wars, found its way over incredible obstacles, and culminated in the formation of the World Council of Churches—an astonishing chapter in Christian history! And yet this climax was the threshold of a new crisis—the one in which we still stand today. Even before the First Assembly met in Amsterdam in 1948, it was becoming painfully clear that our progress had brought us to the point where our residual disagreements began to become more acute as the area of disagreement grew smaller. At Amsterdam there was a good deal of the old familiar tug-of-war between the parties which has so often in the past been the warning signal of breakdown and collapse. Yet this same Assembly also saw a clear focusing of the residual questions which the movement must yet resolve. It also saw a sincere reaffirmation of the covenant of the council: 'We intend to stay together as Christians who acknowledge each other, in some essential sense, as Christians.'

But, the actual existence of a World Council of Churches poses an anomaly which simply has to be faced—and, providentially, can be faced in the community which the World Council of Churches symbolizes. It is, as we have said, not a church—simply 'a fellowship of churches which accepts our Lord Jesus Christ as God and Savior.' This is a *pre-theological* standpoint;

it points to the Christian fact, but does not make its definite meaning clear. The implications drawn from it, particularly in ecclesiology, are by no means uniform or harmonious. It was, therefore, obvious that there were churches in the fellowship unprepared to recognize certain other churches as *fully authentic churches*—and this in spite of their recognition of their members as Christians, 'in some essential sense.' The Orthodox, to cite the extreme case, cannot regard the World Council of Churches as a fellowship of equals—since they regard themselves as the true and irreformable church in which all essential doctrinal questions are settled once and for all by Holy Tradition.[30] But there are also other churches in the Council with serious reservations about the form and praxis of certain other member-churches. Indeed, in widely varying degree, something of this kind may be true of us all.[31]

At Toronto, July 1950, the Central Committee of the Council faced this anomalous situation head-on. A subcommittee on 'The Church, the Churches and the World Council of Churches' canvassed the issues carefully and reported their findings candidly:

The member churches of the World Council of Churches do not necessarily recognize each other as true, healthy or

---

[30] Cf. Hamilcar Alivasatos, op. cit. pp. 49–52.

[31] Cf. articles in *The Christian Century*, May 11, 1949, p. 580; June 8, 1949, p. 700.

complete churches, but they consider the relation of *other* churches to the Una Sancta [their own presumably being settled] as a question for mutual consideration.

This was a fuzzy statement of a literal fact, put too brusquely and without regard for all the facts and feelings involved. This first draft was toned down a bit for the final report, and put in ampler context. It emphasized that the World Council of Churches is not a 'super-church'; that it has no official doctrine of the nature of the church; that its program for overcoming existing divisions is provisional; that it does not prejudge the ways and means to unity. But a basic and inescapable issue had been brought into the open—and many of the 'ecumenical honeymooners' were disturbed and alarmed. It was a tense meeting, with at least a few threats of withdrawal and many dire mutterings.

Yet the Toronto meeting illustrates brilliantly the distinctive genius of the new ecumenical movement and its power to contain the stresses of doctrinal controversy within a community of mutual recognition. One of the wisest and clearest heads in the meeting summed up its meaning in discerning fashion:

'The Toronto meeting undertook to establish the thesis that, on the basis of a common faith in Jesus Christ as God and Savior, a *fellowship* of churches can be built which contains deep differences of belief as to the nature of the church and its unity; furthermore, that no one view of the church must presume to oust any other view from the fellowship, for *all* have equal rights to be there. In the course of the discussion the document was brought to a high degree of precision in formulating these theses, and the fact was revealed, in all its starkness, that such a council demands the mutual commitment in one fellowship of churches which make sharp and painful denials about each others' nature.

We faced it, and we said that we still want *that* kind of council, for 'a very real unity has been discovered in ecumenical meetings which is . . . the most precious element of its life. It exists and we receive it again and again as an unmerited gift from the Lord. We praise God for this foretaste of the unity of his people and continue hopefully with the work to which He has called us together. For the council exists to serve the churches as they prepare to meet their Lord who knows only one flock.' [32]

The crisis at Toronto has been followed by other crises—and there are more to come. But the reality of Christian fellowship has not been broken, the integrity of the ecumenical enterprise has been confirmed, and tempered hopes have been raised at least a little!

A great new event has happened in our time: the restoration of basic Christian community among many Christians who have covenanted to seek the *fullness* of community—*together!* This search must inevitably take

---

[32] Oliver Tomkins, 'The Church, The Churches and The World Council of Churches,' *The Christian Century*, Vol. LXVII, p. 946.

many forms and directions, and in each the necessity for continued, patient doctrinal discussion is basic. Some of these new forms and directions are already becoming clear. Yet no man knows for certain what the Good Shepherd will yet require of us in order for His divided flock to become 'one fold' (John 10:14–16).

The amazing thing—almost a commonplace by now to many, but still amazing—is the subtle but profound transformation of outlook, feeling, and insight which occurs among men and women who have shared deeply in the various kind of ecumenical experiences of work and worship. By caring for the unity God wills for us, we have come to realize the unity He has already given us. By moving toward other Christians in good faith we have begun to realize the primacy of the Christ-Event and the community which depends upon it. We have discovered a new atmosphere in which the imperative to Christian truth prompts the most arduous theological toil—in the confidence that, even now, we may plant and others may water but it is God who is giving the increase. We have already come to belong to a community which does not have to wait upon full doctrinal consensus to begin to enter into the joy of the Christian *koinonia*.

IV

FOUR

The Christian Tradition

THUS far we have argued that the ecumenical movement is the great new fact in contemporary Christianity; that it has served to make Christians aware of their common history; that it has helped to restore the Christian sense of community within which full doctrinal consensus is a goal but not a precondition; that its basic covenant has been shaken and tested, but still holds firm—because the unity we seek has been foretasted in our present fellowship.

But we have also seen that the ecumenical movement is a fellowship of very diverse and divided churches. It is a community still far from full accord. It has entered a critical stage of its development where further progress is bound to be slow. Yet the imperative upon us to go forward remains as strong as ever. And the choice is still as stark: either we maintain our commitments to each other and to God ever more devotedly, or else we must accept their miscarriage as yet another futile gesture toward a professed unity in which we do not really believe.

If the ecumenical movement had begun with an attempt to produce a systematic doctrinal 'confession,' we should never have reached even this present state. Yet the community we have achieved requires of us that we go on to press even harder for broad and deep consensus about our doctrines, our ways of worship, our full communion. This means prolonged, patient, frustrating, difficult theological work—not only by the great and near-great but also by the rank and file of thoughtful Christians throughout the churches. It means that we must seize the opportunity afforded us, within the ecumenical community, of reappraising and recasting our respective traditions in sincere obedience to the highest authority we know as Christians. Anything less than this will stultify our professions, and we shall have only ourselves to blame if our forward motion slows from a march to a shuffle.

None of us can presently foresee all that is involved or that will be required of us in this quest for full consensus. But one thing seems certain from the outset: we shall not get very far if we disjoin Scripture and tradition and set them over against each other. One of the most familiar experiences in ecumenical conversation is the *impasse* created when the same Scripture is interpreted in sharply differing ways because of the different traditions of the interpreters. In such a case, the appeal to *sola Scriptura* is self-deceiving, since it assumes that either we have no conditioning tradition or else that we can abstract ourselves from our traditions in hearing and obeying the Word of God. On the other hand, the usual appeal to church traditions leads to a consequence even worse. For this denies the decisive authority of Scripture and it exalts one church's traditions over the traditions of all the others. Thus we are confronted with the quandary of plural absolutes.

This conflict of traditions may be transcended—but only by the emergence of a new spirit and outlook in the traditionary community. Traditions, especially traditions which divide, can never be simply annulled. We may see this in the relations of the Orthodox in the ecumenical movement on the one hand, and in their relations with Rome on the other. Orthodoxy and Protestantism have many traditions in sharp contrast—and yet their new spirit of mutual recognition (however limited from the Orthodox side) has enabled members of these separated traditions to enrich and be enriched in their ecumenical experience. Orthodoxy and Rome have many traditions in common—and both allow their traditions an authoritative role alongside Scripture. To many Protestants, the breach between Roman and Eastern Christianity appears minor when compared to the gulf between Rome and the Protestants. Yet it is one of the deepest and sorest wounds in

Christendom—and the most ardent zealot for Christian unity cannot conceive an honest way to heal it. Traditions unite and they divide—and the ones that divide are tragically inflexible.

There is simply no blinking the fact of the plurality of traditions among the divided churches. And these traditions tend to keep them divided even when they appeal to Scripture. There is a Lutheran tradition—and it did not cease to develop after Augsburg. In it, Martin Luther is often co-starred with St. Paul. And although the Formula of Concord expressly invokes the *sola Scriptura*, the same formula also speaks of Luther's Catechisms as *Die Laienbibeln* ('the layfolk's Bibles').[1] There is also a Calvinist tradition, furnished with an immense confessional literature which professes to do nothing more than expound Scripture, but does so in a fashion to mark off a highly distinctive Protestant type.[2] There is an Anglican tradition, which exhibits an interesting mixture of catholic and evangelical elements. There is, again, a Methodist tradition, which sprang from its Anglican source but which now, after a century and a half of separation, shows the typical ambivalence of kinship and disinheritance. There is an

---

[1] *The Formula of Concord*, Part First, Introduction III (Jacobs' edition), Vol. I, p. 492.

[2] Cf. Ernst Troeltsch, *The Social Teachings of the Christian Churches* (New York, Macmillan, 1931), II, 576–655.

'Anabaptist' tradition, highly diverse and polymorphous, which constitutes yet another Protestant type—more influential in Anglo-American Christianity than in its European homeland.[3] The notion of a non-traditionary church is a fiction.

Moreover, even if we wished to do so, we cannot simply repudiate our respective pasts. There is no wiping the slate clean, no prospect that one of the currently 'true' churches will persuade the rest of us simply to be swallowed up, *ad gloriam majorem Dei!* Our plural traditions are going to remain plural, in some degree or other, and the fullness of the unity toward which we move must somehow contain them or else it will not be full or real.

But how can we go beyond, or rise above, these plural traditions of ours? Christians share with other human beings the thirst for absolute certitude—and we readily infer from our urgent desire for this that a provident God must have included it among His good gifts to men. We cannot bear the word, 'It is not for you to know times or seasons' (χρόνους ἢ καιρούς), etc. (Acts 1:7). Moreover, this certitude must be extensive and it must be *located*—in an infallible book, an infallible church, an infallible man! And always the infallible norm we seek is something that we can possess, manipu-

---

[3] Cf. my chapter, 'The Reformation and Classical Protestantism' in George F. Thomas, ed., *The Vitality of the Christian Tradition* (New York, Harper, 1944), pp. 116–48.

late, or control. This wish to be exempted from error, to be insured by the infallible, becomes an *obsession*—in the literal sense that a man or church may come to insist on maintaining an absolute rightness in the face of *competing* absolutes and at the cost of unreason and moral outrage. Moreover, religious obsessions are not always mild and innocuous affairs. We know all too well how much blood has been spilled, how many fires have been lit, how many racks have been turned—by Christians, too, in psychopathic 'good conscience.'

Is there an actual and real authority for all Christians which stands above our competing authorities, beyond the reach of our manipulation and control, but genuinely present, actively operative? Is there a center and source of authority which is rooted in concrete fact and Christian history—and yet *not located or circumscribed by human institutions and traditions*? Is there really such a thing as 'the faith once for all delivered [handed over, παραδοθείσῃ] to the saints,' (Jude 1:3)? And is this faith primarily an affair of propositions and beliefs—or is it a dynamic power capable of historical transmission and development?

There *is* just such an authority for *all* Christians. It is the origin and center of our faith and our community. It is God's self-manifestation in Jesus Christ who possesses all men who receive Him (John 1:12). It is God's prime act of *tradition*—or 'handing over' Jesus Christ to share our existence and to effect our salvation. 'For he who did not spare his own Son but 'handed him over' [παρέδωκεν αὐτόν] for us all, will he not also give us all things else with him?' (Romans 8:31-32; cf. also Romans 4:24-25).

This divine 'tradition,' or *paradosis*, was a divine act in human history—and it is renewed and made contemporary in the ongoing course of history by the act of God's Holy Spirit, whom Jesus 'handed over' to his disciples in the last hour on the cross (παρέδωκεν τὸ πνεῦμα John 13:30).[4] The Holy Spirit—'sent by the Father in my name' (John 14:25)—re-creates the original act of tradition (*traditum*) by an act of 'traditioning' (*actus tradendi*), so that the tradition of Jesus Christ becomes a living force in later lives and in faith based on response to a contemporary witness. It is this *actus tradendi* which changes a man's historical knowledge of Jesus Christ—far away and long ago—into vital faith in Jesus Christ—'*my* Lord and *my* God!'[5]

This historical *traditum* is, so to say, brought into the

---

[4] Cf. Hoskyns and Davies, *The Fourth Gospel* (London, Faber and Faber, 1947), p. 532.

[5] Cf. John 14:25–6; 16:12. Professor Franklin Young has pointed out to me that one of the deliberate aims of John's Gospel was to republish the tradition of Jesus so that *Jesus Himself* might be re-presented in the Christian community (cf. John 20:31). This takes place only by the Spirit's action—but Jesus has promised us the Spirit to abide in His church. John is, therefore, demonstrating the power of the Spirit to renew and transmit the original tradition in successive acts of 'traditioning.'

living present by the *actus tradendi*. It looks both to the past and also to the eschatological expectation which gives direction and urgency to Christian life and work in the present. The drama of our salvation points to its fulfillment and climax in Christ's *Parousia*—when the fullness of His victory over death and evil will be made manifest. 'Then comes the end' (τέλος), Paul reminded the Corinthians, 'when [Jesus Christ] will hand back [παραδιδοῖ] the kingdom to God the Father, after having destroyed every other rule and every other authority and power' (I Cor. 15:25; cf. also 15:25-28 and Philippians 3:21). God's deed in Jesus Christ reaches from a point in historical time through our living present to the unpredictable future—and the authority of *God's tradition of Christ* is equally authoritative and final at every point in this line.

God's *traditum* was received by the Apostles and the Church—by the descent of the Spirit which enabled them to be witnesses to Jesus Christ in Jerusalem and in all Judea and Samaria and to the end of the earth (Acts 1:8; cf. 3:22). This testimony to the total Event of Christ—and its saving import—became the essence of the apostolic preaching. What they had received they felt commissioned to hand on to others.

In much the same way, St. Paul—whose apostolic appointment was apocalyptic rather than traditionary (Gal. 1:12)—felt commissioned to hand on what he had received 'from the Lord.' 'For I received from the Lord what I then handed on to you [παρέδωκα ὑμῖν] that on the night in which he was "handed over" [to death], the Lord Jesus took bread... (I Cor. 11:23-25). Again, with regard to the resurrection faith, Paul handed on to his first hearers, as of first importance, what he himself had received, 'that Christ died for our sins, according to the Scriptures' (I Cor. 15:3-11). It is of crucial importance to observe how closely the tradition in Paul and in the Jerusalemite church agree in their essentials. Both owed their origin and authority to the Spirit's *actus tradendi*.

The primary aim of the apostolic community was to 'hand over' Jesus Christ to all who would receive Him by faith and according to their testimony. The supreme authority among them was the Spirit who, by the *actus tradendi*, had brought the *traditum* into living encounter in the church, in its worship and common life. This was the church's center, the source of its unity, the measure of its truth. Their confidence in the Spirit's renewal of the tradition gave to the patristic Christians an amazing sense of being bound by the Holy Spirit to the tradition, and of being free in the Spirit to interpret this tradition and its meaning in new frames and forms as the church continued to move through history, and as she was plunged into successive crises.

Certainly in its early centuries, the Church had to manage without a definitive doctrinal system, without a fixed or uniform liturgy, with only the rudiments of a central organization or a settled polity. It was almost continually embroiled in the struggle with heresy and schism, wracked with the tumult of inner strife and the pressures of the civil state. And yet the scattered churches and their leaders formed a real community and lived in it with solid confidence and hope. Theirs was the *koinonia* of the new age. They were charismatic men who had received the Spirit's power to witness. They were humble men, who knew that they did not themselves possess the power they wielded. All this gave them the authority to re-present God's *traditum* in preaching, liturgy, and ethical teaching. It furnished them guidance in dealing with heresy and schism, in discriminating between a *kerygma* that centered in Jesus Christ as Lord and Savior and any other message that had its center elsewhere. Thus, they could condemn as heresy anything which stultified the original Gospel by distorting either its historical or soteriological reality.

Ignatius of Antioch is something of a prototype of an ecumenical theologian. On his way to a martyr's death in Rome, he rejoices to discover (as in Philadelphia) or to confirm (as in Ephesus and Smyrna) that his fellow bishops and fellow Christians do, in fact, share with him a consensus in the universal faith. This was to be expected, he explains, 'for wherever Jesus Christ is, there is the Catholic church.'[6] The measure of the good

---

[6] Epistle to the Smyrneans, viii. This is the first instance of the phrase 'catholic church' in Christian literature.

bishop—his real authority—is his witness to Jesus Christ. This makes the bishop the proper celebrant of the Eucharist and the visible symbol of the unity of the church.[7]

And it is this, rather than pride of power, which makes Ignatius insist upon the necessity of Christians' being in communion with the bishop as the focus of their unity. Ignatius' own church in Antioch is now without a bishop but in their unity with all other Christians the Antiochene Christians are still secure. For Antioch 'has God for its shepherd' and Jesus Christ as its bishop.[8] The tradition of Jesus Christ, received from the apostles and renewed by the Spirit in the church, gives Christians power and wisdom to repulse heretics and to maintain themselves in fellowship, both in the local congregation and in the church at large. The important—and familiar—doctrinal summaries which Ignatius gives the Trallians (IX) and Syrmeans (I, XII) naturally underscore the actuality of the historical details of the original *traditum*.[9]

The most striking expression of this viewpoint—one of the most interesting in patristic literature—comes in his letter to the Christians in Philadelphia:

---

[7] Epistle to the Philadelphians, iii.

[8] Epistle to the Romans, ix.

[9] See above, p. 71.

I take refuge in the Gospel which, to me, is Jesus-in-the flesh. And I also rest back upon the Apostles, as represented by the continuing presbytery of the Church. Let us also cherish the Prophets, because they foreshadowed the Gospel. They hoped in him (Jesus) and waited for Him and were saved by their faith in Him—and thus they were one with Him. Their message is part and parcel of the Gospel of our common hope . . .

I also trust in the grace of Jesus Christ, who will free you from all bondage. Thus I can exhort you not to act in a partisan spirit, but to follow what you have learned in the school of Christ. When I heard someone say: 'What I do not find in the official records, I do not regard as belonging to the Gospel' and when I answered them, 'It is in the Scriptures,' they retorted, 'But that is just the question!' But so far as I am concerned, Jesus Christ is the sum of all the official records ['Εμοὶ δὲ ἀρχεῖα ἔστιν 'Ιησοῦς Χριστός]; the incontestable records [τὰ ἄθικτα ἀρχεῖα] are his cross and death, his resurrection and faith through Him. By *these* I desire to be justified, thanks to your prayers . . .

The priests are good, but the High Priest is better . . .

He is the door of the Father, through whom Abraham and Isaac and Jacob and the prophets and the Apostles and the Church all enter. All these contribute to union with God. But the Gospel has something unique—the coming of the Savior, our Lord Jesus Christ, His Passion and His resurrection . . . The Gospel is imperishable. It is the fulfillment of the [prophetic] expectation.[10]

The Christian records are—Jesus Christ, come in the flesh! This statement of Ignatius is not in itself a creed, yet it has in it the heart of orthodox faith. Formally, it is a *pre*-theological confession, yet it is the substance of every sound theology. Here is the witness to an encounter with the living God, self-presented—mediated to men from its source in the original act of tradition by the living process of tradition and witness in the church. From this standpoint, everything in the church—its Scriptures and creeds, its liturgy and doctrine, its polity and ethos—all subserve one proper end: 'that men may believe that Jesus is the Christ, the Son of God, and that believing, they may have life in *His name*' (John 20:30).

The patristic church charted its course by its sense of tradition, and it is unanimous in its assumption that the oral tradition of the Apostles and the written tradition of the Scriptures were consilient. The center of Scripture is God's self-presentation in Jesus Christ. The church is the witness to this revelation, and is thus able to interpret Scripture.[11] Scripture is fixed and definite; the tradition is alive and growing. But they are identical

---

[10] *Epistle to the Philadelphians*, iii.

[11] Irenaeus, *Adversus Haereses* II, 41:2; 40:2; V, 20:2.

in content and purpose. They are both given by God to confirm and stengthen one another, and thus to provide Christians with a bifocal vision of the one Word of God which makes them one community.

Tertullian of Carthage, a vivid and eccentric ex-lawyer with one of the most original minds in the history of Christian thought, also emphasizes the Christian tradition as both *traditum* and *actus tradendi.*[12] He carefully distinguishes the Christian tradition—the apostolic faith as it is witnessed to in the living church—from Christian traditions (sometimes termed 'customs,' *consuetudines*). These latter are those varied practices and received forms, both rites and doctrines, which have come to abound in the different churches.[13] They are not without their value, but they cannot be set alongside *the* Christian tradition. 'For our Lord Christ has made himself known to us as the Truth itself, not as Custom.[14]

With unconcealed reluctance, I put by the temptation to examine the array of witnesses to this consilience of tradition and Scripture in the patristic church.[15] It is

---

[12] *De testimonium animae*, v–*a deo traditum est.*

[13] *De praescriptionem hereticorum* 19; *De baptize* 1; *De corona* 3 (4 times); *Ibid.*, 4 (six times); *De jejuno* 10; *Ibid.*, 13 (twice); *De pudicitia* 1.

[14] *De virginibus velandi*, I, i.

[15] But for those who would like to follow this sampling with more comprehensive surveys, Van Leer, *Tradition and Scrip-*

enough here to emphasize that the *first* mode of the apostolic preaching and 'traditioning' was, of course, oral. Later, and quite without formal 'authorization' by the church, the apostolic tradition was 'deposited' in writing—in those Scriptures which the church came, still later, to recognize as the canonical New Testament.[16] In the patristic church as a whole, there is no essential opposition between Scripture, the rule of faith, and the teaching tradition—nor are they ranked in any invidious order. The church is directly bound to the *actus tradendi* in her preaching and worship and, essentially, in the sacraments of baptism and the Eucharist. The church is equally bound to the Scripture for it contains the primitive witness to God's *traditum*. The consilience of Scripture and tradition shapes the

---

ture in the Early Church (Assen, Van Gorcum, 1954), H. E. W. Turner, *The Pattern of Christian Truth* (London, Mowbrays, 1954) are useful for the ante-Nicene period. For the period of the Ecumenical Councils, cf. J. N. D. Kelly, *Early Christian Creeds* (London, Longmans, Green, 1950) and R. V. Sellers, *The Council of Chalcedon* (London, S. P. C. K., 1953). For the scholar, the work that currently overshadows all others is Grillmeier and Bacht, eds., *Das Konzil von Chalkedon, Geschichte und Gegenwart* (Wurzburg, Ekter-Verlag, 1951), 3v.

[16] The familiar claim that the church produced the New Testament can be misleading. The New Testament certainly was produced *in* the church and *for* the church—but not *by* the church, in the sense that the church took any conscious decision to *commission* any of the New Testament writings.

form of the church and guides its forward motion from 'the fullness of time' until 'the end of the age.'

Upborne by this sense of living tradition, the church traveled the enormous distance from its first council (Cf. Acts 15:1-29; Gal. 2:4-21) to the last council which has been commonly counted as ecumenical (II Nicea, A. D. 787)—and beyond. It was an evolution so complex and confused that its historical reconstruction is fantastically difficult. For the journey was traveled in an uproar and the details are downright shocking to the tender-minded. There was scant good will among the controversialists, and once ecclesiastical and imperial politics had pooled their stakes in the struggle, disorder in the church became chronic. It is hard to find, in the whole course of the conciliar period, a single theologian who really tried to understand what his opponents intended to say or who was genuinely interested in enlarging the area of agreement between the contending parties. The malignant strife between Alexandria, Antioch, and Constantinople in the first half of the fifth century did not stem from really irreducible doctrinal issues, but rather from cynical and ruthless breaches of Christian charity and community. Nestorius was not, in real fact, a 'Nestorian.'[17] Cyril was not actually a mono-

---

[17] Cf. G. R. Driver and Leonard Hodgson, *Nestorius, the Bazaar of Heracleides* (Oxford, Clarendon, 1925); see also Aubrey Vine, *An Approach to Christology* (London, Independent Press, 1948).

physite.[18] Leo's *Tome*, at Chalcedon, did not *force* a 'Western' Christology on a reluctant East. Rather it reinforced the strong Antiochene and Constantinopolitan traditions still powerful in Eastern Christianity, but which had been eclipsed and overthrown by the Alexandrines at the Latrocinium ('the Robber Synod' of Ephesus, A. D. 449).[19] In their contentiousness, Christians mistook their separate traditions for God's *traditum* in Christ and thus brought the bonds of their Christian *koinonia* under intolerable strain.

Yet the astonishing thing is that, despite the shoddy performance of the bishops, the erratic interference of the emperors, the demented violence of the mobs of monks, the sad discrepancies between official and vulgar Christianity—despite all this, the actual dogmatic results were, in every case, far better than the operating procedures would seem to account for.

The core of the conciliar decisions continue in the line of the apostolic tradition. This was, indeed, their sole justification. They secured for the church both the fullness and the mystery of God's deed in Jesus Christ. We cannot here survey the shaping of the Christological dogma. I can only record my conviction—which I

---

[18] R. V. Sellers, *Two Ancient Christologies* (London, S. P. C. K., 1940).

[19] Cf. R. V. Sellers, *The Council of Chalcedon*, pp. 110–19; 265ff.; 341ff.; 228–53.

intend to substantiate elsewhere—that the positive outcome of this shameful chaos was a good deal better than was once the fashion to admit. The ecumenical creeds, for all their strange—and non-Biblical!—vocabulary, managed to do the essential thing. They affirmed and ratified the heart and soul of the Christian tradition. They laid it down beyond cavil that our salvation is from God Himself; that Jesus Christ is the one true mediator of this salvation; that in the Mediator faith recognizes *both* his full and actual deity *and* his full and actual humanity. It was the priceless service of the Chalcedonian definition that it held the church both to its historical *traditum* and to its living experience of *actus tradendi*. Moreover, it insisted that the former is the measure of the latter. Any result short of this would have made of Christianity an unhistorical ideology (as in monophysitism) or else it would have compromised one or the other of the two basic New Testament Christological motifs: the one that, quite certainly, Jesus Christ was a man 'in every respect tempted as we are, yet without sinning' (Hebrews 4:15; cf. 5:2), and the other, equally certain, that, 'in [Jesus Christ] all the fullness of God was pleased to dwell and through him to reconcile all things unto himself' (Colossians 1:19-20).

We are suggesting that the development of the Trinitarian and Christological dogmas was an integral expansion of the original tradition and its revelation of the nature and purposes of God. We know, of course, that many 'radical Protestants' have seen in this development only a disaster—a falling away from Biblical simplicity and a miscarriage of the mission of the primitive church. Yet, their own theologizing is noticeably retrograde when they seek to interpret the New Testament in 'nondogmatic' fashion.

From a different quarter, many 'liberal Protestants' (e. g. Harnack and McGiffert) have viewed this traditionary development as a distortion of the essential ethical message of primitive Christianity, which was, in Harnack's famous 'definition': 'Eternal life in the midst of time, under the eye and by the power of God.'[20] McGiffert regarded the metaphysical speculations of the conciliar period as thoroughly alien to the nature and intention of the early church.[21]

Yet again, and more recently, Professor Martin Werner of Bern has denounced the outcome of the evolution of dogma. What came to be 'orthodoxy,' he argues, flourished in direct ratio to the waning of the primitive Gospel. The prolongation of history forced the church to *de-eschatologize* its original Messianic expectations. But into eschatology's place there came a doctrinal outlook which had little, if anything, to do with New

---

[20] Adolf von Harnack, *What is Christianity?* (New York, Putnam, 1901), p. 8.

[21] A. C. McGiffert, *A History of Christian Thought* (New York, Scribner, 1953), I, 275, 289.

Testament Christianity. Orthodox Christianity, says Werner, is *ersatz* Christianity:

As a substitute for primitive Christianity, orthodoxy produced what finally came to be known in the Middle Ages as Christendom: a hellenistic-syncretistic mystery religion, promenading about in Christian clothes (*in christlichen Gewande einhergehende*), but all musty with the decadence of all that post-classical religiosity.[22]

We cannot stop to debate this obviously complex issue—except to point out that there is something profoundly unhistorical about this notion that we might cancel the interim centuries and then somehow manage to recover New Testament Christianity intact and undefiled. Besides, Professor Turner has already furnished us with a splendid refutation of all these primitivist contentions.[23] What matters most to us at the moment is the question of the authority of the creeds and councils. One might even agree with their detractors that their authority is not intrinsic. But one ought to go on to point out that they, themselves, appeal beyond themselves—*to the Scripture* AND *the tradition*. Their authority rests on their power to re-present Jesus Christ—and God's

---

[22] Martin Werner, *Die Enstehung des christlichen Dogmas* (Bern, Leipzig, P. Haupt, 1941), p. 725.

[23] H. E. W. Turner, op. cit.; see especially chapter VI.

saving grace in and through Him. But this is the authority of *any* doctrine, *any* creed, *any* liturgy, *any* tradition.

If we are agreed—with allowable reservations and amendments as to the way I have put it—that the heart of the ecumenical dogmas rings true to the Christian tradition, what follows? Might not the church have achieved the same result by holding simply and unswervingly to the text and terms of Scripture? The answer here is that where it tried to do just that, it failed—for not only the Devil but heretics and schismatics can quote Scripture for their own purposes. Dangerous and confusing as the process was, the church was forced to utilize alien categories (current in the thought-world of the time) in order to *preserve the basic intention of the original message*. The Greek categories which they borrowed—*ousia*, *hypostasis*, *prosopon*, *physis*, and so on—were egregiously ill-suited to the purposes of explicating the concrete vividness of God's *Self*-revealing in Jesus Christ. But, for good or ill, they were the best analytic notions available to the Greek fathers. We may seek better interpretive categories—and we ought to—but we must not forget why we need interpretive categories of any kind: that we may receive God's tradition in its original vitality and intelligibility—and have it renewed for us by His Spirit in the living community.

Yet, if we accept the conciliar dogmas as integral to

the Christian tradition, are we also obliged to accept the whole mass of the traditions, canons and cultus of the patristic church? Must we all, as a condition of holding the whole faith in sincerity, approve also the invocation of the saints, the cult of the Virgin, the patristic liturgical forms, the sacerdotal distinction between clergy and laity, etc., etc.? If this be the case, then the prospects of full consensus on the plural traditions of the ancient church are poor indeed. For if *all* ancient traditions stand or fall *en bloc*, by what principle could we avoid adding the Western medieval traditions, and the continuing additions by which modern Rome enlarges the ancient traditions: the dogmas of Immaculate Conception, Bodily Assumption—and, presently, *Maria Co-Redemptrix?* The only constructive answer is to measure *all* the various traditions of any and every church by the single Christian tradition. By this standard, we might find a way to discriminate between those additive traditions which *are* necessary to the effectual transmission of the Christian tradition, and those which are indifferent, superfluous, or misleading.

If our hope for unity is more than wishful thinking, we must acquire the habit of referring all our theologizing to the one, singular, and supreme tradition of God in Jesus Christ—witnessed to in Scripture, received, renewed, and transmitted by the Spirit in the church. This *traditum* stands above all the traditions of its interpretation and expression, whether in Scripture or in the church. All Scripture and every church tradition must be measured by this concrete reality: *do they re-present Jesus Christ, as He was and is and shall be, to the eyes of faith, to the mind and heart of love?*

Martin Luther found the Gospel again in the Scripture—and often seemed simply to equate the Scripture and the Gospel. Yet deeper than this formal reliance on Scripture, which was largely an apologetic position in the face of Roman claims, was his Christocentric understanding of every aspect of faith and grace and life. In his famous criticism of the Epistle of James, he states his norm for appraising Scripture:

> Another reason [for judging this Epistle not apostolic] is that although [James] would teach Christ's people, he pays no attention to the sufferings, the resurrection or the Spirit of Christ Himself. He mentions Christ several times, but he does not teach much about Him. Instead, he speaks in general terms about faith in God. But the business of the true apostle is to preach Christ's passion, resurrection and saving office, and to lay the foundation on which others may stand with him—just as Christ said: 'You shall be my witness' (John 15:27). And here is the essential agreement of all the authentic holy books, that together they preach Christ and call men to Him. This is also the proper criterion (*Prüfestein*) for criticizing any book. Look to see if it calls men to Christ or not, since all Scripture testifies of Christ (Romans 3:21) and St. Paul will know nothing but

Christ (I Cor. 2:2). What does not teach Christ is not apostolic even if St. Peter or St. Paul were doing the teaching. On the other hand, whatever preaches Christ is apostolic even if Judas, Hannas, Pilate or Herod were doing the preaching.[24]

All the great Reformation watchwords—*sola Scriptura, sola fide, sola gratia*—have one essential meaning: *solus Christus*. This is the source and center of Christian faith—and it is only when this faith is hardened into disparate doctrinal systems, and the systems substituted for living faith, that community disintegrates. *Solus Christus* is the content of Christian theology and it is the source and center of Christian community. When theology loses its clarity on this point and community loses catholicity in this center, then disagreements of every other sort may become just grounds for division.

Solus Christus is also the measure of the permissible boundaries of Christian teaching, for all the actual heresies in the history of the church are Christological aberrations and *mis*-re-presentations of Christ. *Jesus Christ is the Christian dogma*. Everything else in Christian thought derives from or subserves this primordial conviction. And the Christian tradition has, as its sole function, to bring men into living encounter with Jesus Christ, as He truly was and is, and so bring them to-

---

[24] *Vorrede auf die Episteln S. Jacobi und Juda.* (*Luthers Werke*, Erlangen edition 63, pp. 156–57).

gether in His Body, the church. As Daniel Jenkins has put it:

> Scripture shows that what constitutes the Church as the Church is the presence in its midst of God through the living Christ in the fellowship of the Spirit. The existence of the Church arises directly out of the ministry of Jesus Christ.[25]

And, we might add, so does the continued existence of the church, in its unity and catholicity. The authentic power and authority of the church depends upon and derives from its effectual witness to the *traditum* which was its origin and to the *actus tradendi*, which is the continual miracle of its ongoing life.

The authority of the Scripture does not derive from the authority which its authors claimed for themselves—for some notoriously silly apocryphal literature bears the same external claim. The New Testament is 'the sole and sufficient rule of faith and practice' because of its witness to Christ and its agreement with the apostolic preaching. The authority of the church does not rest on its own claims to privilege—as guardian of the tradition, as possessor of Scripture, or keeper of the keys. These claims must be measured, and are in some sense measureable, by the church's faithful transmission of

---

[25] *The Strangeness of the Church* (Garden City, N. Y., Doubleday, 1955), p. 62.

the tradition of Jesus Christ and by the agreement of her total tradition with the deposit of this tradition in Scripture. The authority of doctrine does not rest on its claim to summarize either Scripture or church tradition—but on its actual efficacy in 'the public portrayal of Jesus Christ as crucified and resurrected before [men's] very eyes' (Gal. 3:1). The unity of Christians cannot be achieved by their yearning toward each other—but only through their attentive obedience to the Word of God in Christ Jesus.

Something like this, I suggest, has actually been present among Christians from the very beginning and in every age right into the present. In wide diversity, in tragic division, in times of decadence and revival, in different cultures and diverse intellectual climates, Christians are rightly named only when they have responded to the tradition of God's act in Jesus Christ and are sharing in the community called out by this act and thrust through time by its eschatological import. This is *the* Christian tradition in the church—both *traditum* and *actus tradendi.* Its acknowledgment and embodiment gives the church its only authority and its only true unity.

This Christian tradition measures all its media. From it we may learn to discriminate between the essentials and the nonessentials in our doctrines and polities (i. e. what belongs to the faithful transmission of *the* tradition) between what belongs to the church's very essence (i. e. the receiving and transmitting of *the* tradition) and what belongs to the church's most effective ordering, worship, and common life. If our first loyalty is to the Christian tradition, we can appraise the plural traditions of the divided churches with deeper understanding and clearer insight, and so come to see how unity in the Christian tradition allows for a manageable diversity and pluralism in Christian tradition*s* of various sorts. We could see which are the essential doctrines (dogmas) and which, in the freedom of the Spirit, are matters of choice and taste among the Christian traditions, forms, and customs. In short, we should find that in the Christian tradition there is unity which neither seeks nor allows dead-level uniformity.

For all their exaltation of Scripture, Protestants have known–deep down–that Jesus Christ is the Lord of Scripture, and that Biblicism smacks of the 'old law.'[26] For all their exaltation of the church, Catholics know that Jesus Christ is the Lord of the Church, and the Scripture is the decisive witness to His Lordship.[27] The church has the right and power to judge the actual enemies of the Christian community, even when they quote Scripture or invoke rival traditions, but the

---

[26] Cf. the conclusion of the *Westminster Confession*, ch. I, Of the Holy Scripture, x, Schaff, *Creeds of Christendom*, III, 605–6.

[27] Even Rome denies that the Church is the author of Scripture. Cf. Decrees of the Vatican Council, *De Revelatione*, Schaff, op. cit., II, 214–42.

church's measure is not itself, but the Christian tradition and the consilient witness to this tradition in Scripture and our common Christian history.

Some such perspective as this lies behind the famous 'canon' of Vincent of Lerins—developed, incidentally, in partial reaction to the doctrinal extremes of the greatest Christian doctor of them all, St. Augustine.[28] For Vincent, the unity of the church depended on its steadfast maintenance of the Christian traditions:

Because of the profundity of Holy Scripture, not all its readers receive its meaning in one and the same sense. One interprets its words in one way and another understands its words in yet another. It almost seems that Scripture yields as many interpretations as there are interpreters . . . Therefore it is quite necessary that the rule for interpreting the prophetic and apostolic writings must be framed in accordance with the basic sense found in the ecclesiastical and catholic traditions. Moreover, within the Catholic Church great care must be taken that we all hold fast to *that which has been believed everywhere, always and by everybody*. This is truly and strictly what the term catholic means. . . .[29]

---

28 Cf. my chapter, 'The Person and Work of Jesus Christ' in Battenhouse (ed.) *A Companion to the Study of St. Augustine* (New York, Oxford, 1954), p. 359ff.

29 Patrologia latina, v. 50. col. 610. Cf. *Vincent of Lerins*, trans. by R. E. Morris in *Fathers of the Church*, v, VII, p. 270.

But what *has* been so believed? What else beyond the revelation of God in Jesus Christ by the Spirit through the church? In the nature of the case, the plural and divergent traditions of the separated churches will not qualify under the canon of *quod ubique et semper et ab omnibus!* The Vincentian canon could not be directly applied to the solution of a single outstanding doctrinal controversy among the divided churches today. But when we look at these same separated churches, we cannot deny of most of them, at any rate, that their best intent is to receive God's gift in Christ, to have it renewed in faithful hearts at worship and work, and to hand it on as evangel to all who will hear and heed. And if there are churches which are doing this imperfectly, inadequately, ineffectively, still it is by *this* standard that they can be judged and reformed, and must be willing to be judged and reformed.

By such a 'norm,' we could go on cherishing many of our several traditions, just so long as we do not confuse them with *the* Christian tradition. We could recognize the typical faults of the traditionary process—that traditions tend to 'run down' in the course of time,[30]

---

[30] Cf. some interesting comments on this point in Sigmund Mowinckel, *Prophecy and Tradition* (Oslo, J. Dbywad, 1946), p. 30ff.; in Francis Hare, *Church Authority Vindicated* (London, J. Roberts, 1719), pp. 38–9; and in Edward Stillingfleet, *Scripture and Tradition Compared*, in a sermon preached at Guildhall Chapel, November 27, 1687 (London, printed for H. Mortlock, 1688).

that they are inevitably additive, that they produce vested guardians of traditions who identify themselves with the traditions they are set to guard. We could recognize the danger of traditions which are affirmed as infallible and irreformable. This recognition in itself would greatly reduce the danger of 'traditionalism.' It would also greatly enhance the possibility of the continual reformation of church traditions by the measure of the Christian tradition.

There is simply no prospect whatever that we shall reduce the different church traditions to a universal uniformity. What is more, the Christian community would be much the poorer if it should lose a large diversity in its traditions—of doctrine, liturgy, and polity. What matters is that it be *diversity-in-unity*, and that the unity shall center in our common loyalty to God's 'tradition' of Jesus Christ and to the Spirit's 'traditioning' of Jesus Christ in the church. This is the unity which we have received, which even now we know in foretaste. The further fullness of this unity turns upon our willingness to move toward the Center of our community—the Head of our one Body—in order that we may move closer to one another!

This is what the ecumenical movement has begun to do. The basis of its membership points simply and directly to the Christian tradition: 'a fellowship of churches which confesses our Lord Jesus Christ as God and Savior.' Nothing more—nothing less! Is this not a reassertion of a primacy long since lost when churches tried to bring all their traditions with them into the unity they sought. Within the World Council of Churches there are many different traditions of the most diverse sorts, many of them having very little to do with *the* Christian tradition. But the World Council of Churches does not—and ought not—pass such a judgment. It cannot recommend the rejection of any existing doctrine or praxis in any member-church. But it can, and should, call all of them firmly and constantly to consider—together—the measure and the import of the Christian tradition.

Membership in the Council puts many searching questions to our plural church traditions: How faithfully and how adequately does this particular tradition call men to Christ? Or, does it actually call them to itself, ignoring or contemning the other sheep of His one fold? Do our traditions serve to enliven and enrich faith, or do they present some law, some cult, some abstraction, some *substitute for faith?* Do they liberate men from their insularities and exclusiveness to make them catholic Christians, in Ignatius's literal sense of members of the *whole* Body of Christ? [31] Does this tradition or that practice bring men to a vivid sense of the unity of God's truth and the diversity of men's expression of it? Does it prompt men to speak 'the truth in love, . . . to grow up in every way into Him who is

[31] See above, p. 114.

the head, into Christ, from whom the whole body, joined and knit together by every joint with which it is supplied, when each part is working properly, makes bodily growth and upbuilds itself and love' (Ephesians 4:15-16)?

We must not forget, indeed, that Jesus poured out his scorn upon 'the traditions of men' (Mt. 15; Mark 7), and against those who mistook these traditions for the weightier matters of the Law (cf. Mt. 23:23). The Reformers had warrant for denouncing and deploring the *traditiones humanae*.[32] These warnings are in good order wherever men confuse pious custom or established usage with their first and ultimate faith. Still, this does not cancel the value of traditions which do subordinate themselves faithfully and ecumenically to *the* Christian tradition. Both in the New Testament, and in subsequent ages, we see pluralism in theological patterns, in liturgical forms, in polity and order. All of this is acknowledged in the ecumenical movement as part of the richness and complexity of the Christian community.

Nothing is more striking, in an ecumenical gathering, than the diversity of doctrines and rites there represented. And one of the distinctive features of such a setting is the added richness which this diversity gives

---

[32] Augsburg Confession, II, v, in Schaff, op. cit., III, 42–9; First Helvetic Confession, Art. IV, in Schaff, op. cit., III, 212; Second Helvetic Confession, II, iv–vi (ibid., III, 239–40).

both to discussion and the experience of worship and common action. If *the* Christian tradition is to be effectively handed on to *all* sorts and conditions of men, there must be many different modes and means of its transmission—but all of them must be aimed at and measured by their common and identical end. The unity of the church does not lie in the uniformity of her doctrines and rites, but in the unity of her witness to her common Lord—and to His Lordship in all of life.

God's first act of tradition was given at a particular point in time. The Spirit's 'traditioning' takes place at a later time, so making the bridge between that particular 'then' and any subsequent 'now.' And this divine relation of that point in past time with every living now constitutes the historical process of the church's continued existence. No simple repetition of the story of the original act of tradition suffices to call men to God in Christ. And yet, unless this *traditum* stands before men, supported by competent and faithful witnesses, the Spirit's act of renewal does not occur. The genius of the Scripture is that here we have forever the primitive witness to the original act of tradition, and the first account of the Spirit's act of renewal. Scripture tells us both of our Savior and of the creation of the community of our salvation. The genius of tradition is that it has the power of the renewal of this event in succeeding ages, so that men in *any* age may stand as close to the original event as did the first converts at Pentecost!

All member churches in the World Council of Churches stand before *the* Christian tradition, and confess it, in one way or the other, as the one authority above their plural traditions. They do this, in some degree, in their separate church life, as one of the requirements of their participation in the ecumenical movement. This confession—'of Jesus Christ as God and Savior'—does not mean the same thing to all the different confessors. These differences run deep and involve complex, far-reaching consequences. Yet it is the task and the opportunity of the ecumenical movement to confront its members with the question as to whether these outstanding differences in interpretation are deep enough and wide enough to justify continued division between their churches. No prejudged answer must be given until this confrontation has gone on long enough to plumb the depths of the issues involved. But we have the opportunity for such an exploration just because there is already among us some measure of identical recognition and confession of the Christian tradition which bespeaks our unity and entitles us to recognize one another as Christians.

The Scriptures bear witness to this unifying tradition—they body it forth. Our common Christian history bears witness to this unitary tradition. It is the dynamic medium of its transmission through the ages. Even our divided churches bear witness to the one Christ and this is the source of the *vestigium ecclesiae* in each of them.

This is another way of saying that God's Spirit has

never left the church which He brought forth, and which He continues to sustain and upbuild. This is why men who acknowledge the gifts and fruits of the Spirit in others must recognize that in so doing they are recognizing the Christian tradition as their matrix and medium. This is why men who cherish their own traditions may expect of the Spirit, who 'authorizes' Scripture and judges our traditions, that He will lead us to a point where we can successfully resolve the discrepancies which we may be led to see between our traditions and *the* tradition. The genius of the ecumenical movement is that we do not have to have in advance a detailed blueprint of the unity we seek. It suffices us to have experienced the foretaste of that unity and to believe that the quest for unity is an act of obedience to Him whose manifest will is that we all shall be one.

The ecumenical experience has supplied countless thousands of Christians with some sort of experience of what this means—in common worship, in common action, in urgent practical projects, in common endeavor in theological work. It may very well be that there are those among us who know more certainly than the rest of us what the final shape of the restored Christian community is to be like. The rest of us will not readily learn from their confident assertions. Our only way is the way of ecumenical persuasion—ecumenical experience in the ecumenical community, in the spirit of the Christian tradition.

When we review the results of the last five decades—

the alteration of the ecclesiastical climate, the actual unions and reunions that have taken place, the scores of active negotiations actually under way, the emergence of united churches on many continents, the slow, steady build-up of ecumenical influence in many quarters of the churches, etc., etc., the impression grows that this whole movement has been led in ways past the wisest planning of its best leaders. This is both a judgment and a consolation. A judgment because we have accomplished far less than was possible. A consolation because we have already accomplished far more than many of us would have dared to hope for.

As we face into the oncoming phrases of the ecumenical movement, which is almost certainly going to be more difficult than its earlier phases, what matters most is that we shall become even more fully aware of the community that we actually *have*, even clearer than we are now as to the reality of our common Christian history. This done, we shall find ourselves in the right atmosphere for our continuing work together; we shall have a footing for our hope that we can find our way from our separate standpoints to the vital Center of our common faith. From here, the way will open toward a more substantial consensus in faith and doctrine, worship and common life.

Given such a temper and such an outlook, the whole company of Christians could join in the quest for understanding and agreement. We could then continue to work away at our presently 'insoluble problems' with a confidence born of hope, an expectation begotten of actual experience. The way to Christian unity is by way of the Source of that unity, and in the community in which the Spirit still bestows His gifts and fruits.

In the little seaport town of Ystad, in the south of Sweden, there is a lovely old church built by the Franciscans in the fourteenth century. There was little iconoclasm in the Swedish Reformation, and this church, like many others of its general period, has survived almost intact. It has a rather conventional altar, with crucifix and choir, and the pulpit is attached to a pillar down in the nave—a fairly typical design. But directly across from the pulpit on the opposite pillar, not more than thirty feet away, hangs another crucifix, life-size and vividly life-like, with human hair matted under the crown of actual thorns. When I visited the church in 1952, I naturally asked about this second crucifix, for I had never seen a similar arrangement. The story, as it turned out, goes back to a visit to Ystad, and to this Mariakyrchen, of the great warrior hero king, Charles XII, in 1716. The visit was unexpected, and the pastor was so overwhelmed by this sudden burst of glory that he put aside his prescribed text and substituted an ardent eulogy of the king and the royal family. Some few months later, the Church received a gift from King Charles. It was this second crucifix, and with it these instructions: 'This is to hang on the pillar opposite the pulpit so that all who shall stand there will be reminded of their proper subject.'

In the ecumenical gatherings I have attended, there has been much ado about protocol and organization. The opening sessions are full of forced good-will, adroit maneuver, a fair amount of head-knocking, and no little posturing. But in every one of them, there has come a time–unplanned and unexpected–when we did become aware of our proper Subject, and a new spirit rose among us. Somehow we became open to Christ's Spirit in our midst, really aware of the group as 'members one of another.' Our sense of community was renewed and ratified, and we could go on about our business with a new sense of direction and goal. As long as this sort of thing continues to happen, we can be sure that this is God's work, in which He is bringing to fruition, better than we know how to receive it, that unity for which we work and pray!

V

FIVE

The Unity We Seek

'FOR me, the sum of the records is Jesus Christ.[1]' This quaint confession of Antioch's ancient martyr-bishop points us to the vital substance of the New Testament and our common Christian history. Whatever measure of community we have—or can have—is community-in-Christ. And the measure of all our doctrines, our liturgies, our polities—and our ecumenical aims!—is their faithfulness to the Christian tradition of God-in-Christ. Our separate traditions can be justified only insofar as they truly represent, to us and others, the Christian tradition, to be received, renewed, and transmitted. Our only hope for unity-yet-to-be-achieved lies in the acknowledgment of the unity-already-given by

---

[1] See above, p. 116.

God in Christ. This discovery that the future imperative to unity derives from the present indicative of unity is one of the really crucial impulses of the modern ecumenical movement.

All this would seem obvious, self-evident—and much too simple! Even if divided Christians were to affirm it all, would this really solve our difficulties? Does it yield any particular doctrine of the person and work of Jesus Christ—or of the church, the ministry, and the sacraments—which would cut through the tangle of denial, rejection, and confusion that besets us now? Does a pious word about Jesus Christ contribute anything of real importance to ecumenical discussion or negotiation? Has our whole argument, then, not fallen prey to sentimentalism and theological naïveté?

This last question is calculated to make a theologian shudder. For he knows that his reputation could more easily stand the charge of heresy than the suspicion of naïveté. So strong is the habit of doctrinal analysis upon us all that the essential simplicity of the Gospel cannot be borne until we have converted the *kerygma* into a set of propositions and these, in turn, into a corpus of doctrine and ritual. Yet one of the plainer lessons of Christian history is that one of the prime sources of theological renewal is the return to the pre-theological reality of faith—the faith which springs up in the encounter with Christ. I have as much interest as any other theologian in a sound Christology, an adequate ecclesiology, a proper doctrine of the sacraments and the Christian ministry. The temptation to propose what I would regard as good answers to these questions is naturally a strong one. Yet there are two good reasons—beside my own limitations—for resisting such a temptation. The first is that these very problems are currently being worked through by a host of ecumenically minded theologians, singly and in concert—and the fruit of all these efforts is not yet ready for harvest. The second is that even when the harvest is in, it will spoil unless the churches are ready to receive it in a mood generated by what we have called 'the ecumenical atmosphere.'

Let us be clear, then, as to the nature of our undertaking in these lectures. Throughout them we have been pointing to the distinction between the ecumenical *atmosphere* and an ecumenical *blueprint*, between the posture of faith and its conceptual outworkings. We have asserted that the doctrinal tasks of the ecumenical movement—crucial as they are—must be conceived in the right order of Christ-Event, Christian community, Christian doctrine. We have insisted that all men and churches who sincerely confess Jesus Christ as God and Savior belong in the Christian *koinonia*, share our common Christian history. There is not, at present, a universal doctrinal consensus or cultus, but there is a community in which these can be sought without supposing that uniformity is the same as unity. And there is, increasingly, a common admission that our common task is to receive and transmit the witness of God's saving deed in Christ. Until we have appropriated the full significance of *what we already have in common*—God-given!—we cannot hope to proceed to the *fullness* of unity. And this we have not yet done.

From the beginning, the ecumenical movement has sought to widen and deepen the fellowship of Christians in service, worship, and understanding. One of its aims is doctrinal consensus in a sacramental community. But we deceive ourselves if we suppose that what we are waiting for—in order to get ahead—is an ecclesiological formulary so neat, so ingenious, and so imposing that we can all assent to it and then move easily into the ecumenical age! The time is not yet ripe for any such sort of theological 'break through'—and is not likely to be until we have gone on living and working and worshiping together a good while longer and a good deal more seriously. There is still a long uncharted road before us in our pilgrim journey toward the unity we seek. And the rules of the road must include at least the following: *force no issue; avoid none; eyes center!*

This is not a counsel of indecision, nor a sentimental reliance on some principle of assured progress. We have stressed the fact that the ecumenical movement is at a very critical point—where many another effort at unity has failed before! Our problem then is to weigh our difficulties in the balance of our resources. And our chief resource is obviously the unity God has never withdrawn from us even when we have been withdrawing from each other. The barriers between us will fall in good time—in God's time!—if meanwhile we have continued at our proper business. And this means laying our separate traditions alongside the Christian tradition and learning therefrom what is really essential in our own and in the others. If we do this in good faith, we can then be hopeful of the future, confident that by ways not now predictable, the Holy Spirit will convert our present impasse into an open thoroughfare.

Now that 'the ecumenical honeymoon' is over, and the momentum of ecumenical progress has slackened somewhat, we are able to see more clearly than before the resistances within the churches toward the ecumenical enterprise. They have always been present, but now their nature and power are more plainly discernible in contrast to what positive impulses there are toward unity.

There is, first of all, the force of *inertia* which operates in the churches almost as in physical bodies, to keep them in their state of constant rest or motion unless acted upon from outside. We all know the force of familiarity, and the threat of the unfamiliar. It encourages us to hold fast to what has seemed good, to cherish the patterns which have ministered to our spiritual life, to ignore, or to regard with critical reserve, the strange and alien forms of other traditions. Since we believe, in all sincerity, that our churches are, respectively, authentic members of the Body of Christ, we are all too easily content to continue as we have been—open and cordial toward all others, but fundamentally preoccupied with our own affairs. An ecclesiastical leader may be loyal to the ecumenical movement, may accept office or responsibility in it, but he rarely finds it 'possible' to devote even a large fraction of his time, energy, or creative genius to the cause of unity, as compared with his service in the maintenance of his own denomination. The vast majority of churchmen are favorably disposed toward ecumenicity—indeed, it is rather bad form nowadays openly to oppose it! But the obvious concern of the overwhelming majority of us is still with the fortunes of our own particular church and the influence of our church among the churches. It may very well be, as we have argued, that unity will come as a sort of by-product of real faithfulness in the churches—but as long as the ecumenical movement is a side-issue to the average churchman, the hope of its success is deferred.

Resistance to wholehearted ecumenical effort comes also from a very different source. This is *despair of any real or final success.* There are many of us who know how heavy the weight of Christian history is against the hope of Christian unity. And we have seen, in ecumenical work, how subtly and powerfully the forces of self-sufficiency, competitiveness, and reaction work to dampen our ardor for understanding and mutuality. We have often been depressed—or offended—by the lack of charity among the brethren when sharp issues are sharply defined by the ugly discrepancies between profession and performance in ecumenical negotiations. We are hypersensitive, and defensive, about the depth and complexity of our difficulties and the intransigence of conscientious men. If unity comes at all, it will have to be a sheer miracle—and our faith in the likelihood of such a miracle is, at most, fainthearted.

But the most powerful resistance to unity comes from *fear*—fear of losing cherished gains and values in our own traditions, the fear of reckless change. For even if we are willing to see the *status quo* altered, we are still apprehensive lest the alteration be too drastic or go too far. This feeling is widespread—and not altogether unwarranted. False unity *can* be bought too cheaply. A good while ago (1914) Ronald Knox (still then an Anglican) expressed this fear in an amusing, malicious essay consciously modeled on the style of Jonathan Swift. He entitled it *Reunion All Round, or Jael's Hammer Laid Aside, and the Milk of Human Kindness Beaten up into Butter and Served in a Lordly Dish—Being a Plea for the Inclusion within the Church of England of all Mahometans, Jews, Buddhists, Brahmins, Papists and Atheists, submitted to the consideration of the British Public.*[2] The argument of this sparkling satire, stripped bare, is that if you modify *any* of the distinctive Anglican traditions, there is then no further barrier to 'reunion all round.' Not only would there be

---

[2] London, printed by Charles Jacobi, for Samuel Gurney, and sold by the Society of SS. Peter and Paul at 32 George Street, Hanover Square, MCMXIV.

room, in such a conglomeration, for nonconformists but for any and all sectaries—in short, for everybody, including the uttermost extremes: the papists and the atheists! This, one is supposed to conclude, is absurd. The presumptive conclusion follows: we must not, therefore, modify *any* of our distinctive Anglican traditions! It may be only incidental to remark that Knox has lived by his own logic. He is now a Roman Monsignor!

This fear of the loss of identity is deep in us all. We cherish our own traditions, and with good cause, for it was from them that we received the Christian tradition. In any synthesis of traditions, much may be lost of great worth, not only to ourselves but to the fullness of the community. The churches in the Catholic tradition fear that they may be asked to surrender the essentials of Holy Tradition—and their fear is warranted insofar as they insist that *all* their traditions are ingredient in Holy Tradition. The Reformation churches have a fear that they may be asked to compromise the *sola Scriptura;* and their fear is warranted insofar as they insist that their dogmatic standards are co-equal with Scripture. The so-called 'Free Churches' have a fear of being swallowed up by the traditionalist churches and of losing their Christian liberty in faith and order, polity and church life. Their fear is warranted insofar as they cherish the notion of diversity-in-unity even more than that of unity-in-diversity!

There *is* risk to the churches in the ecumenical movement. The explicit assumption of our fellowship is that our present disunity must be overcome. But the implicit assumption of the movement strikes even nearer home: if disunity is to be overcome, all of us are going to be altered, in some degree or other, in the process. *All* our traditions are on trial in the ecumenical community and we have not yet learned to apply the measure of *the* Christian tradition properly to place them within that unity which we are seeking. This cannot help but be disquieting.

There is no formula that will banish these resistances of inertia, despair, and fear. But they might be reduced somewhat if we can catch a vision of what sort of unity we are after or believe to be imperative for us. It will do us no good to plot a blueprint or chart of 'the coming great church,' but it ought to be possible, even now, to indicate some of the insights and goals which prompt our quest. Indeed, this very question is the theme of the first North American Conference on Faith and Order, to be held in Oberlin in September 1957. As a part of the preparation for this conference a widespread and fruitful exploration of this theme is already under way. My comments here are offered as a modest share in that greater venture.[3]

First and foremost, *the unity we are seeking is the fullness—and the fulfillment—of the unity that we have.*

---

[3] Cf. my article, 'The Unity We Have' in *The Christian Century*, June 13, 1956, vol. 73, pp. 720–22.

We cannot seek for what we do not know at all. And if we already know, even in part, the reality and joy of unity-in-Christ, then it is from that concrete, present experience that we must learn about the fullness of unity which we do not yet know. It is fruitless—and un-Biblical—to speculate about the ideal church in some Platonic heaven or even on some Aristotelian earth! Our quest for unity begins where we are, in our divided churches, but it begins with an experienced reality of Christian community within and among those churches. Let us then look at some of the features of this unity which we have already experienced, even if only in partial and ambiguous terms. From these we can perhaps descry a prospect of that fuller unity which would overcome our resistances.

Already we know at least a partial unity *in faith and teaching*, which can almost certainly be developed into doctrinal consensus if we are patient, faithful, and open. In the early days of Faith and Order, it was widely feared that the chasms between the churches went so deep as to leave little common substance in their faith. And yet the almost constant result of Faith and Order conferences has been the discovery that our common faith is deeper than our disagreements, both in substance and even in expression. The great themes of Biblical and creedal faith are shared by churches of the most diverse liturgies and polities. The depth of evangelical fervor is not the monopoly of the 'Evangelicals.' When we have explained to each other what we mean by our theological words and liturgical actions, more often than not, we have encountered intelligent understanding—and criticism! But the criticism itself would be impossible without a common ground. In the capital elements of the doctrines of God, Jesus Christ, the Holy Spirit, man, sin, and grace, the great bulk of ecumenical theologians would already agree more than they would differ. And the discovery of this agreement has supplied the incentive to push deeper and further into the residual disagreements. In many ways, this has been the most audacious and successful of the ecumenical projects.

Again, we seek *a unity in Christian hope*, for we have already experienced the power and uplift of that insight into the meaning of Christian hope which we have already come to share. As most of us know, the Second Assembly of the World Council (Evanston, 1954) centered its entire program around the theme, 'Jesus Christ—the Hope of the World.' When this theme was chosen, there were some misgivings as to its fruitfulness. It pinched many a sensitive nerve, exposed awkward differences between 'European' and 'American' theology, confronted many people with the unfamiliar word and notion of eschatology, and forcibly raised the crucial question about Christian faith and expectation.

In the preliminary work for Evanston, there was a great deal of confusion and tension—some of it quite serious. Just before the Assembly met, *The Christian Century* deplored its choice of theme and foresaw 'an elpidological [*elpis* is the Greek word for hope] fogbank closing in on the shores of Lake Michigan.' One cannot report that this forecast was wholly wrong, either. The Assembly's wrestling with its high theme was something less than a resounding triumph. And yet, no single event in the Council's history has done so much to demonstrate the common footing beneath the swirling tides of theological confusion. Evanston helped us all to realize, more vividly than we had done before, that our hope is in Jesus Christ, that He *is* the hope of the world. One leading church official recently remarked that before Evanston, he had never paid any serious attention to the term eschatology—and regularly associated it with the familiar highway signs 'Jesus is coming soon!' and the apocalyptic advertisements of the 'hot gospellers.' At Evanston, he said, the term and notion took on a whole new world of meaning for him. The Christian hope, as he came to understand it there, has now become the most dynamic element in his thinking. In a distraught and demoralized age, the Christian hope which we presently share prompts us to seek its fullness, together with the whole Christian community—and to share it with the human community.

Again, we are seeking a fullness in our unity of *Christian worship* because we have found that the unity we already know in worship is one of the most precious values in our ecumenical experience. This is the widest and most nearly invariable agreement among all who have participated in ecumenical conferences. This past summer it was my privilege to share in a three-week

Theological Students Seminar at the Ecumenical Institute at Celigny near Geneva. The members of the seminar were from eighteen countries and nearly thirty denominations, Orthodox, Anglican, and Protestant. It was decided that for each of the three weeks we would use for our vespers a single ritual: Anglican Evensong for the first week, the Orthodox Vesper Litany for the second, and a Reformed service for the third. Each of these forms was explained and discussed in the seminar before we began the series. At the end of the seminar nearly everyone agreed that our worship had been the most significant part of our ecumenical experience. I well remember an American Methodist theolog, after the first evening of the Orthodox Litany muttering to me: 'I don't get it. It seems terribly archaic!' In his written evaluation, two weeks later, he noted the Orthodox vespers as the high point of the entire seminar. Obviously, this sort of enthusiasm cloaks a multitude of difficulties. But, even so, there are already so many of us who *know* the reality of ecumenical worship that its fullness becomes a deeply cherished goal in the unity we seek.

Any unity in worship among Christians, however, must mean *a sacramental community*—and this, too, belongs to the unity we already have, albeit in tragic ambiguity. For one thing, we have discovered that the limits of sacramental communion are already wider than we had supposed—and some former limits have been surmounted. For another thing, we have faced up squarely to the fact of the pain and heartache which divisions at the Lord's Table must rightly cause. We now recognize that the sacraments and their 'due administration' is perhaps the sorest of all our problems. Yet even here, candor and openness have led us to see a present unity which bears the promise of something yet greater. The well-nigh universal recognition of the validity of baptism in the member-churches of the World Council is a broad and firm foundation in our present unity. We have not yet found a way to a truly common Eucharist for us all, but we know that this is the final ground on which we aim one good day to stand. Thus, it is heartening to a constant increase in the concern and longing for a sacramental community, a font and a Table where all may feel at home and *be* at home.

A sacramental community entails some sort of *common and representative ministry*. Here is where the accidents of our separate histories face us with many harsh realities. None of the churches will deny outright the necessity of some kind of historic continuity in the ministry—but is there *any* church whose 'succession' has *not* been called into question? Does the universal fact of schism leave the orders of any of us *completely* unscathed? This is a fearfully ticklish point, for every one of us has a defense and apology for his existing ministerial order—and some of these *are* more plausible than others. The real problem, however, is not how we can defend the existing situation but whether we can move beyond it. How this may be done is not fully plain. Yet, again, even in this thorniest of the ecumenical brambles, the unity we have points toward the fullness of the unity we seek. There is an increasing number of churchmen in the Catholic tradition who hesitate to deny *all* validity to the ministry of 'those in irregular orders,' who are willing to acknowledge *some* signs of the gifts and blessing of the Holy Spirit in the exercise of such 'defectively ordered' ministries. There is at least some sophistry in the argument that the demand for reordination does not imply *any* repudiation of a man's first orders. And there is manifest pride in the scornful counter-claim that the 'regularity' of ministerial order does not matter. But the fact that such explanations are being offered suggests that our situation, though anomalous, is not hopeless. The unity we seek is one in which ordination to the office and work of priest and minister in the church of God means—just that. And the experience of the Church of South India in this regard suggests that the barriers to such an achievement are not as insuperable as many of us had thought.

Finally, we seek a *unity in love*, God's love which calls out our love for all our brethren. In the ordeal of ecumenical work, we have discovered a bond between us which resists the abrasions and absorbs the heat generated by our zeal for the truth. This is something rather different from friendship and personal intimacy, for ecumenical contacts are typically cursory and episodic. It is something quite different from the amiability of like-minded people, for ecumenical gatherings are often more motley than Pentecost. It is God's *agape*, which calls out our love and turns it into understanding and devotion (I John 4:10). It is a love which casts out fear and lays on us an imperative to unity, and a measure of our obedience:[4]

> Behold, if God so loved us, we also ought to love one another. . . . And we know we have passed from death to life because we love the brethren. He who does not love remains in death.

There are manifold corruptions of love in our ecumenical endeavors, and a fair amount of hypocrisy. But the reality of the love we have experienced makes us know that the *fullness* of this love would truly be 'the joy of our Lord.'

The unity we seek, therefore, is not something wholly unknown or ideal. We have foretasted it, and we have recognized that its source and end is Jesus Christ. The progress from where we are to where we aim to go does not require any relocation of the Center of our faith, any redefinition of our common Christian history. And if this is so, and so long as it remains so, we can expect and accept further changes and mutations

---

[4] I John 4:11, 3:14.

in our corporate life. We might even welcome them, with the liberty of Christian men, who are bound to the *traditio Christi* but free from the obligatory force of the *traditiones humanae.*

The program of the World Council of Churches is designed to promote and guide the process that leads toward this fullness of Christian unity. It does so in many ways. It cannot act as a church nor apart from the consent of the member-churches—but it can and does encourage exploratory discussions and actual negotiations between the churches. It works for solutions to various extraneous issues affecting church relations (e. g. proselytism) and its program of ecumenical action covers a wide range of service and study projects. It sponsors ecumenical assemblies, conferences, an ecumenical graduate school, numerous laymen's retreats, and seminars for theological students. The Study Department which includes Faith and Order conducts extensive projects, including four theological Study commissions, one on Christ and His Church, one on Ways of Worship, one on Tradition and Traditions, and one on Institutionalism. In these various study projects, the Council enlists the active interest of theologians and churchmen of all the churches—and the very study process turns out to be an ecumenical experience of major dimension.

The impact of the ecumenical movement within the churches is beginning to be widely felt as more and more churchmen are involved in the various levels of the movement—international, national, and local. It is, of course, the member-churches who must support the work of the World Council and the interaction between the Council and the churches is one of the most critical issues in this present phase of the movement.

But for all that has been done and is being done, there is much more that is needed. The most constant and urgent need is simply *more* widespread and sustained ecumenical experience. The churches must respond to the stimuli of the ecumenical movement *as churches* —and this means using or finding means to interpret the movement and its challenge *to the rank and file of their membership*. What is more, the large and representative ecumenical conferences will have a steadily declining relevance unless the intervals are filled in by regional and local ecumenical study and action projects —among the clergy and laymen, in the universities and theological schools. The path to unity may be *blazed* by a few dedicated, prophetic souls, but the fullness of unity requires that the *whole* people of God be led forward, in knowledge and understanding, in the power of the Holy Spirit.

All that is being done in the ecumenical movement —and all that can be done—is only a mode of faithful 'waiting,' an openness to receive that unity which God wills for us. Unity will come, if at all, less from our zeal and diplomacy than from our deepened understanding, our renewed wills, our awakened love. When we have brought our own traditions and treasures as gifts to the whole family of God—willing no longer to contend for them or for the final outcome—we shall then be ready to receive God's gift of true fellowship in the Christian tradition, which breaks down the walls of partition between us and overcomes our inertia, despair, and fear.

After a hard winter, the spring is often slow to come. Thaws are partial and are followed by late freezes. The going is often harder than in the steady cold. The eager farmer may plow or plant too soon and lose his labor. The hibernants may miscalculate the proper time for their emergence. The raw winds of controversy and conflict may seem worse than their snug winter quarters. But as the vernal signs increase, hope keeps building, discomforts seem incidental to a greater good, and the elation of new life and power springs up.

The Christian community has lived through an unconscionably long night of hibernation and isolation. And now a 'thaw' has come and hope arises that the winter of the Christian soul is passing. Many of us have ventured abroad and have found others of like heart and mind, of whose existence and worth we had never really known. Have we come to a springtime in Christian history? The signs are mixed and confusing. There have been so many times before when hopes revived for a season—and then so many dismal failures. Even now, there is still ground for much misgiving: as to the real temper of the churches, as to the wisdom and effectiveness of certain ecumenical policies. But the hopeful signs increase, the cause is supremely worthful, success has become a credible, though not imminent, prospect.

Will the modern ecumenical movement come to the fruition of its aims in this century or the next? Can we afford to risk our cherished traditions by sharing in this vast ferment of ecumenical life and action? The answer which the churches may give to these questions may finally be, 'No!' But we must recognize that if this happens, we shall not then be merely where we were—but rather in a much worse plight. The shock of disenchantment will force the churches back into their ancient garths, and the cause of Christianity in the modern world will be irreparably weakened. For if the ecumenical vision is quixotic, then the pretensions of the separated churches are certainly no less so.

But what if the churches *maintain* their present affirmative attitudes? In that case, we can confidently predict that two or three generations hence, the Christian community will wonder at our feeble faith, our timidity, our intransigence, our dim vision of what then can be seen to have been feasible all along.

The Christian world has a wager thrust upon it—not unlike Pascal's famous wager of personal faith. Of the two possibilities—that the ecumenical movement is a quixotic distraction or that it is the growing edge of the Christian community—none can infallibly foreknow which is the true judgment. Therefore, wager we must, for whatever we do—or even if we try to do nothing!—we shall be putting our weight in one balance or the other. What matters most, then, is that our choice be made in the full light of conscience and knowledge. This is why the ecumenical movement exists—to provide significant experimental data for thoughtful and serious people so that they can decide, *responsibly*. It is our best hope that divided Christianity will come to realize that what we have known of Christian fellowship—good as it is—is not enough, that we have been too long content with less than God wills for us. The unity we now have is the good that is the enemy of the best, which would be the *fullness* of this same unity in faith and order, life and work .

What is at stake is the Gospel itself—and the honesty and the power of the Christian message. If we *are* 'no longer strangers and sojourners, but . . . fellow citizens with the saints and members of the household of God,' then we *must* 'grow together into a holy temple in the Lord' (Eph. 2:19-20). Only in such a unity, can we speak and do the truth in love and grow up into Him who is our head, into Christ—who was and is and shall be Lord of life, of the Scriptures and the Church (Eph. 4:11-16).

And now to him who by the power at work within us is able to do far more abundantly than all that we ask or think, to him be glory in the Church and in Christ Jesus, to all generations, for ever and ever. Amen. (Idem 4:20).